The Hopi

Indians of North America

Heritage Edition

Indians
of North
America

The Cherokees

The Choctaw

The Comanche

The Hopi

The Iroquois

The Mohawk

The Teton Sioux

Heritage Edition

Indians
of North
America

The
Hopi

Nancy Bonvillain

Foreword by
Ada E. Deer
University of Wisconsin-Madison

CHELSEA HOUSE
PUBLISHERS
A Haights Cross Communications Company

Philadelphia

COVER: Early twentieth-century Hopi bowl, housed in the Newark Museum, Newark, New Jersey.

CHELSEA HOUSE PUBLISHERS

VP, NEW PRODUCT DEVELOPMENT   Sally Cheney
DIRECTOR OF PRODUCTION   Kim Shinners
CREATIVE MANAGER   Takeshi Takahashi
MANUFACTURING MANAGER   Diann Grasse

Staff for THE HOPI

EXECUTIVE EDITOR   Lee Marcott
EDITOR   Christian Green
PRODUCTION EDITOR   Noelle Nardone
PHOTO EDITOR   Sarah Bloom
SERIES AND COVER DESIGNER   Keith Trego
LAYOUT   21st Century Publishing and Communications, Inc.

©2005 by Chelsea House Publishers,
a subsidiary of Haights Cross Communications.
All rights reserved. Printed and bound in the United States of America.

A Haights Cross Communications Company

www.chelseahouse.com

First Printing

9 8 7 6 5 4 3 2 1

Library of Congress Cataloging-in-Publication Data

Bonvillain, Nancy
   The Hopi/Nancy Bonvillain
      p. cm. — (Indians of North America, revised)
Includes bibliographical references and index.
   ISBN 0-7910-7990-2 — ISBN 0-7910-8350-0 (pbk.)
   1. Hopi Indians—History. 2. Hopi Indians—Social life and customs. I. Title.
II. Series.
E99.H7B66 2004
979.1004'97458—dc22

2004004698

Contents

Foreword

Ada E. Deer

American Indians are an integral part of our nation's life and history. Yet most Americans think of their Indian neighbors as stereotypes; they are woefully uninformed about them as fellow humans. They know little about the history, culture, and contributions of Native people. In this new millennium, it is essential for every American to know, understand, and share in our common heritage. The Cherokee teacher, the Mohawk steelworker, and the Ojibwe writer all express their tribal heritage while living in mainstream America.

The revised INDIANS OF NORTH AMERICA series, which focuses on some of the continent's larger tribes, provides the reader with an accurate perspective that will better equip him/her to live and work in today's world. Each tribe has a unique history and culture, and knowledge of individual tribes is essential to understanding the Indian experience.

Prior to the arrival of Columbus in 1492, scholars estimate the Native population north of the Rio Grande ranged from seven to twenty-five million people who spoke more than three hundred different languages. It has been estimated that ninety percent of the Native population was wiped out by disease, war, relocation, and starvation. Today there are more than 567 tribes, which have a total population of more than two million. When Columbus arrived in the Bahamas, the Arawak Indians greeted him with gifts, friendship, and hospitality. He noted their ignorance of guns and swords and wrote they could easily be overtaken with fifty men and made to do whatever he wished. This unresolved clash in perspectives continues to this day.

A holistic view recognizing the connections of all people, the land, and animals pervades the life and thinking of Native people. These core values—respect for each other and all living things; honoring the elders; caring, sharing, and living in balance with nature; and using not abusing the land and its resources— have sustained Native people for thousands of years.

American Indians are recognized in the U.S. Constitution. They are the only group in this country who has a distinctive *political* relationship with the federal government. This relation-ship is based on the U.S. Constitution, treaties, court decisions, and attorney-general opinions. Through the treaty process, millions of acres of land were ceded *to* the U.S. government *by* the tribes. In return, the United States agreed to provide protection, health care, education, and other services. All 377 treaties were broken by the United States. Yet treaties are the supreme law of the land as stated in the U.S. Constitution and are still valid. Treaties made more than one hundred years ago uphold tribal rights to hunt, fish, and gather.

Since 1778, when the first treaty was signed with the Lenni-Lenape, tribal sovereignty has been recognized and a government-to-government relationship was established. This concept of tribal power and authority has continuously been misunderstood by the general public and undermined by the states. In a series of court decisions in the 1830s, Chief Justice John Marshall described tribes as "domestic dependent nations." This status is not easily understood by most people and is rejected by state governments who often ignore and/or challenge tribal sovereignty. Sadly, many individual Indians and tribal governments do not understand the powers and limitations of tribal sovereignty. An overarching fact is that Congress has plenary, or absolute, power over Indians and can exercise this sweeping power at any time. Thus, sovereignty is tenuous.

Since the July 8, 1970, message President Richard Nixon issued to Congress in which he emphasized "self-determination without termination," tribes have re-emerged and have utilized the opportunities presented by the passage of major legislation such as the American Indian Tribal College Act (1971), Indian Education Act (1972), Indian Education and Self-Determination Act (1975), American Indian Health Care Improvement Act (1976), Indian Child Welfare Act (1978), American Indian Religious Freedom Act (1978), Indian Gaming Regulatory Act (1988), and Native American Graves Preservation and Repatriation Act (1990). Each of these laws has enabled tribes to exercise many facets of their sovereignty and consequently has resulted in many clashes and controversies with the states and the general public. However, tribes now have more access to and can afford attorneys to protect their rights and assets.

Under provisions of these laws, many Indian tribes reclaimed power over their children's education with the establishment of tribal schools and thirty-one tribal colleges. Many Indian children have been rescued from the foster-care system. More tribal people are freely practicing their traditional religions. Tribes with gaming revenue have raised their standard of living with improved housing, schools, health clinics, and other benefits. Ancestors' bones have been reclaimed and properly buried. All of these laws affect and involve the federal, state, and local governments as well as individual citizens.

Tribes are no longer people of the past. They are major players in today's economic and political arenas; contributing millions of dollars to the states under the gaming compacts and supporting political candidates. Each of the tribes in INDIANS OF NORTH AMERICA demonstrates remarkable endurance, strength, and adaptability. They are buying land, teaching their language and culture, and creating and expanding their economic base, while developing their people and making decisions for future generations. Tribes will continue to exist, survive, and thrive.

Ada E. Deer
University of Wisconsin-Madison
June 2004

1

The Emergence

Long ago, say the Hopi Indians, the earth was covered with water. There was no dry ground. No animals roamed the mountains and plains, no birds flew in the air, and no people lived. But inside the darkened earth dwelled deities and spirits with great knowledge and power.

One day, the goddess of the east and the goddess of the west decided to create living things. They fashioned a bird out of clay and breathed life into it. The bird flew all over the earth but could find no other living creatures. So the goddesses took more clay and made human beings. They gave the people breath and language and sent them on their way.

At that time, the people dwelled inside the earth. At first, their lives were happy and peaceful. They planted their crops and went about their daily tasks. Then discord arose among the people. They gossiped about each other and argued about many things. Adding to the people's troubles, the rains diminished and the crops ceased to grow. The wisest leaders of the people knew that they must find a way out. Perhaps they could discover a hole in the surface of the ground so that they could escape from the turmoil below.

Soon, one of the chiefs found a ladder made of reeds, which led up to a hole in the earth. He and the other chiefs led their relatives up the ladder and onto the surface. Each chief carried with him a sacred ear of corn that he intended to plant wherever he and his kin eventually settled.

The people were glad to emerge from the earth, but they did not know where to make their homes. The chiefs decided to go in separate directions, each accompanied by his followers. They traveled in the four cardinal directions, going north, west, south, and east. After a long time searching, they each found a good place to stay. Happy in their new homeland, the Hopis constructed villages and began to plant crops. And of greatest importance, they pledged to forever recite the prayers and perform the rituals that the powerful deities had given to them when they emerged from the earth.

This story of creation, told by the Hopis since time immemorial, sets out their fundamental principles of life and order in the world. It also gives the people an understanding of the eternal meaning of their beliefs and rituals.

The name *Hopi* means "good in every respect" or "good, peaceable, wise, and knowing." The word captures the essence of the people's desire for wisdom, goodness, and peace. The Hopis have attempted to establish a way of living that puts these great ideals into practice. Above all, they desire harmony, balance, and order in their relationships with the world and with other people, creatures, and the forces—such as, according to Hopi belief, the gods, goddesses, and spirits—that share the earth with them.

The Hopis strive to live with their families and neighbors according to these ideals of peace and cooperation. They believe that people should help one another, be generous and kind to those in need, and be friendly and good-natured to all.

The Hopis believe that harmony with the natural world comes from knowing one's place in the order of the universe, from knowing that one is a part of the world. People have no right to harm the earth or the creatures living on it but instead should show respect for all of nature's beings.

The physical universe of the Hopis is bound by four horizontal directions—north, south, east, and west; and by two additional directions—up and down. The points of the four cardinal directions are determined by the four farthest points on the horizon marked by the sun as it rises and sets throughout its yearly cycle of summer and winter solstices. (Actually, from a non-Hopi point of view, these directions would be more accurately described as northwest, southwest, southeast, and northeast.) From their present-day home in the southwestern United States, the Hopis consider the territory marked off by these points on the horizon to be their ancestral homeland, found centuries ago by the first human beings.

Each direction is associated with a specific color: north is yellow, west is blue, south is red, and east is white. The zenith (upward) is black and the nadir (downward) is speckled with all colors. Links between directions and colors are especially important in the performance of ceremonies. Designs woven into clothing or painted on ritual objects are colored to signify the directions. Through this use of color to symbolize directions, the Hopis recreate the balance and order of the universe.

Each of the six directions is also associated with a specific animal and bird that can be used together in rituals to represent order in the world. The pairings are:

North: mountain lion; oriole

West: bear; bluebird

South: wildcat; parrot

East: wolf; magpie

Zenith: (no animal); tanager

Nadir: mole; (no bird)

In addition to maintaining balance with other people and with the physical world, the Hopis strive for harmony with the world of spirits and mythic beings. To show their respect for spirits, the people recite prayers, make offerings, and perform ceremonies dedicated to deities and the forces of nature. When the Hopis perform their rituals, they believe they are reenacting the deeds of the first humans, who were directly instructed by the gods. Hopi religious practices therefore link them both to the spirits and to their own ancestors.

In the Hopi view, prayers and rituals are based on principles of reciprocity. People recite prayers to spirits, giving them thanks for their blessing and support. Spirits return the honor by giving the Hopis the aid they have requested.

The Hopis think of life and time as continually transforming. Things that appear to be opposites are just different aspects of a continuous, alternating reality. Hopi beliefs about life and death are good examples of this philosophy. When a person dies, the Hopis believe that she or he is born into another world, the world of spirits. At the conclusion of funerals, the Hopis symbolically separate the realms of life and death by drawing four lines of charcoal on the ground as the deceased's body is carried out of the village for burial. A prayer is recited, telling the spirit of the deceased not to harm the living but instead to give blessings just as the living honor the dead.

When a Hopi man or woman dies, a mask made of white cotton is placed over the face. It is called a white cloud mask and symbolizes the clouds that bring rain to Hopi lands. The Hopis believe that the souls of the dead are gradually transformed into clouds and mist. The souls become a liquid essence that is manifested as rain. People pray to the dead, their ancestors, to bless them with the rain that nourishes their crops and ensures their survival.

Beliefs about death thus reveal several themes basic to the Hopis' religion. Life and death are in a continual process of change and transformation. The Hopis believe that reciprocal relations exist between the living and the dead. Through prayers, people honor their ancestors, and through the gift of rain, ancestors make it possible for the living to survive. It is a deeply poetic image of the continuity of bonds created between people and eternally maintained.

Religious practices are central to the Hopis' daily and yearly activities. Indeed, religion is the bedrock of Hopi *culture.*

Religious ceremonies are held in a special building, called a *kiva* (KEY-va). A kiva is a rectangular structure built completely or partially underground. In either case, it is entered from a trapdoor in the top. A ladder inside the kiva, symbolic of the ladder the first human beings used to emerge onto the earth's surface, descends to the floor, which is divided into two sections. An elevated area provides a place for the public to assemble and observe the ceremonies conducted by ritual practitioners in the lower floor area. On the lower level, a round hole in the ground represents the place where the Hopi ancestors emerged at the time of creation. In other words, kivas symbolize the earth and are a potent reminder to the Hopis of their origins.

In addition to the main room where rituals are performed, kivas usually contain a small room where people store ritual gear such as costumes, masks, and musical instruments used during ceremonies.

Hopi rituals usually last eight days, divided into two sets of four. There is also a preliminary day for participants to

Hopi religious ceremonies are held in kivas—rectangular structures that are either completely or partially underground. Worshippers enter through a trapdoor atop the kiva and a ladder leads into the main room where ceremonies are held.

prepare their costumes and ceremonial objects and to rehearse their songs and dances. During the first four days of each ceremony, secret rites take place inside the kiva. These events are attended only by the villagers who are actively involved in the ceremony. The participants smoke tobacco pipes, producing clouds of smoke that represent the rain clouds so greatly desired. Worshipers also make offerings and recite prayers to the deities.

Ritual participants erect altars in the kiva consisting of vertical wooden or stone slabs that are painted with designs symbolizing corn, lightning, clouds, and various mythic figures. Ceremonial objects are placed before the altar. Among these is a medicine bowl containing fresh spring water. It is set on the ground in the middle of a painting made from colored grains of sand. The sand painting depicts spirit beings whose aid is requested by the people. Around the painting, six lines are drawn with different-colored cornmeal to represent the six directions. Altars and ceremonial objects remain in place during the entire period when the ritual is being performed, but on the next to last day, the altar is dismantled, the sand painting is erased, and the ritual objects are put away for safekeeping.

The second set of four days, or second half of each ceremony, is devoted to public dances and festivities. Some of these activities take place in the kiva and may be attended by adult members of the community. Others occur in open plazas in the village and are viewed by all. Public rituals are lively events. Everyone enjoys listening to the beautiful music and songs and watching the skilled dancers. It is also a time of feasting, socializing, and renewing of friendship and community bonds.

Throughout all the days devoted to a ceremony, ritual participants must observe a number of taboos, or restrictions, on their behavior. They must abstain from sexual activity, and they are not permitted to eat any salt or meat. At night, they sleep in the kiva, away from the distractions of everyday life. These restrictions are also in place for four days after the ritual.

On the last day of a ceremony, participants conduct a rite of purification, sprinkling ashes on themselves and on the special objects used in the ceremony. The Hopis believe that the spiritual powers that have come to them during the religious ceremonies are dangerous if they are treated casually. Therefore, when ritual practitioners return to normal life, they must purify themselves to avoid getting sick from the strength of the powers with which they have come in contact.

Hopi ceremonies occur at fixed times throughout the year. The ritual calendar is divided into two equal periods. One begins in late January or early February and lasts until the middle of July. The other occupies the remaining months until the cycle is renewed the following year. Each period contains a different set of ceremonies. Ritual leaders choose specific dates for most rituals by observing the sun's position as it rises over particular landmarks on the horizon. Some rites are timed in accordance with the phases of the moon.

During the time from February through July, most of the rituals concern a group of spirit beings called *kachinas* (ka-CHEE-nahs). Kachinas are the spirits of ancestors. They are believed to live in mountains on the borders of Hopi territory. The Hopis recite prayers and give offerings to the kachinas so that they will aid their human descendants, especially by bringing the rain that is so vital to their crops.

On certain religious occasions, Hopi men impersonate kachina spirits and appear in Hopi villages, where they are honored at ceremonies. When kachinas visit the people, they are dressed in colorful costumes and jewelry. Their heads are covered with beautiful masks and large headdresses adorned with feathers. Some kachinas take the form of animals or birds, such as the owl, the eagle, and the bear. Others are named after a distinctive feature of their appearance, such as the Long-Bearded or the Left-Handed. While they visit the Hopis, kachinas give presents of food and other items to the villagers, who respond with thanks and prayers.

Kachinas enter villages at sunrise. They proceed in a line led by their ritual father. The kachinas follow a path made of cornmeal, advancing with dance steps to the kivas, where they will be honored by the villagers. Ritual leaders await the kachinas in the kiva and conduct ceremonies dedicated to these ancestral spirits. Other adults may enter the kiva and observe the rites. Children who have been initiated into the kiva may also attend.

During the period of kachina rituals, initiations are conducted for girls and boys to make them members of the kiva society. Children are initiated when they are between six and nine years old. The rites are held each spring for groups of children who have reached the appropriate age. Parents begin by choosing a ceremonial mother or ceremonial father for their daughter or son. Sponsors prepare the children for membership in a kiva by teaching them about their duties as a participant in the society. Later, at the appointed time, the sponsor leads the child to the kiva for initiation.

The initiation rite, called *kachinvaki*, consists of prayers and songs that teach children about the spirit world. In addition, boys and girls are encouraged to behave properly, to treat other people with kindness, and to respect and honor the spirits. Then, the masked kachinas make their appearance in the kiva. One of the kachinas carries branches of yucca, a plant that grows wild in the desert. Another kachina takes a yucca branch and whips each of the children in turn. The young children are frightened to be in the presence of these powerful spirits. But at the end of the ritual, when the kachina figures take off their masks, the children see that the kachinas standing before them are actually their relatives and neighbors.

Ritual leaders explain to the children that even though living people may impersonate kachina spirits, the kachinas themselves watch and approve the proceedings. The powerful essence of the real kachinas comes to the Hopis even though it is embodied by human beings. This is perhaps the most important religious lesson revealed to children at their initiation. They learn that spiritual power affects humans even though it cannot be seen.

The last major ritual of the kachina cycle is called *Niman*. It occurs in mid-July. Niman signals the departure of the kachinas, who leave the Hopis to return to their spirit world. Niman is a festive dance at which people bid farewell to the kachinas for the year. The kachinas reciprocate the people's good wishes by distributing toys to all the children. Girls receive wooden dolls dressed in kachina costumes and masks. Boys are given bows and arrows.

Before the kachinas depart from the villages, a special prayer is recited to them:

> When you return to your homes bring this message to them that, without delay, they may have mercy for us with their liquid essence [rain] so that all things will grow and life may be bountiful.

This prayer reaffirms, once again, the eternal bond between the kachinas, the ancestral spirits, and their human descendants. The Hopis believe that just as they need the kachinas, the kachinas need the Hopis. This is in part the basis for the belief that if the Hopis fulfill their responsibilities toward the kachinas, then the kachinas will fulfill their responsibilities toward the Hopis by sending rain.

After the period of kachina rituals ends in July, a new cycle of religious ceremonies begins. Several different festivals take place, each of which is organized and conducted by members of various ritual societies. People become members of these societies by going through a rite of initiation. During initiations, people learn their duties as members of the society. They are taught the prayers, songs, and dances that they will perform at the ceremonies.

The first ritual performed is the Snake and Antelope festival. Snake and Antelope ceremonies occur in alternate years. Each consists of dances and races conducted by members of the Snake and Antelope societies. The Flute Society performs its own ritual dances in late summer.

In autumn, women's ritual societies conduct three separate ceremonies called Maraw, Lakan, and Owaqol. They are primarily concerned with ensuring women's fertility and the fertility of corn, the earth, and all the plants.

Next, come the rituals of the four men's societies. Their names are Wuwuchim, Agave, Horn, and Singers. Wuwuchim is the most important of the men's rituals. It includes an elaborate initiation rite, beginning with a ceremonial lighting

The Snake Dance is one of the most recognized Hopi ceremonies. The first eight days of the sixteen-day ceremony are spent gathering snakes, which are washed and purified. During the dance, the snakes serve as messengers to carry the Hopis' prayer for rain to the spirit beings.

of a new fire to symbolize a boy's new birth into the society. After Wuwuchim, the other men's rituals are performed. Agave is dedicated to success in war; the Horn Dance is directed at ensuring a good hunting season; and the Singers ritual is concerned with human fertility.

Finally, the last ritual of the yearly cycle occurs each December at the time of the winter solstice. It is called Soyal, and its purpose is to renew the earth and the life-giving forces upon which the Hopis depend. During Soyal, painted wooden sticks, called prayer sticks, are buried in the ground. They contain prayers that the Hopis believe help maintain the universe and ensure the earth's bounty. (For additional information on these religious rituals, enter "Hopi ceremonies" into any search engine and browse the many sites listed.)

In addition to the society members who organize and participate in specific ceremonies, ritual clowns play a very important role in the public part of many religious festivals. Clowns are men who dress in brightly colored costumes and paint their bodies and faces with intricate designs. Clowns entertain observers with their comic imitations of animals, birds, and people. They may speak in riddles, shout obscenities, or tease bystanders.

But Hopi clowns also mete out discipline and warnings to people in the community who have behaved inappropriately and have injured their neighbors. Perhaps someone in the village is known to be uncooperative, lazy, or argumentative. Such an individual may be singled out by a clown during a public ritual. The clown then loudly ridicules and insults the wrongdoer in the presence of all onlookers. He may spill a pail of water on his target or even whip the offender with tree branches. This public confrontation usually makes targets feel ashamed and leads them to change their behavior.

Finally, clowns serve the purpose of teaching people about the limits of acceptable human behavior by giving a negative example. Clowns do outrageous things that are not permitted for ordinary people. They may use obscene language, imitate sexual acts, and even urinate or defecate in public. Such actions are, of course, intolerable in normal society. But by shocking people with their behavior, clowns teach the rules of proper social living. Their behavior is tolerated because they are considered deities and are thus sacred. The Hopis also understand that they are reversing normal behavior: This is what it means to be a clown. Although the Hopi villagers may be surprised and entertained by the clowns' antics, they also are reminded of cultural norms of etiquette shared by members of the community.

Hopi attitudes toward religion include both actions and thoughts. The Hopis believe that conducting rituals, performing sacred dances and songs, and reciting prayers help establish harmony and balance in the universe. Through these activities, the Hopis show respect to deities and spirit beings. And in return, spirits bestow blessings and bounty on the people. But in addition to performing the proper actions, people must have a "good heart." To the Hopis, this means controlling one's emotions, being kind to others, and keeping one's thoughts focused on peace and harmony.

2

Origins

The Southwest region of the United States has been inhabited by Native Americans for at least ten thousand years. Over many millennia, these peoples developed cultures that relied on nearby natural resources for food and equipment. The Hopi tribe is one of numerous Indian groups descended from the original inhabitants of the Southwest. Hopi culture shares many characteristic features with other peoples known collectively by Europeans and Americans as the Pueblo Indians. They are called this because the Spanish word *pueblo* means "town." It is the word the Spaniards used for the Hopi and similar Indian *tribes* who lived in permanent villages of multistoried adobe dwellings.

The Southwest is majestic, endowed with mountains, desert lands, plateaus, *mesas*, and deep canyons. It rises high above sea level to altitudes of five thousand to seven thousand feet. The climate is arid, with rainfall averaging only between ten and fifteen inches per year. There are also relatively few permanently flowing rivers in the Southwest. The lack of both rain and flowing water makes survival in the region extremely difficult. Despite the harshness of the environment, many forms of plant and animal life have been able to adapt. The desert contains many varieties of natural vegetation, including roots, grasses, plants, and cacti. Juniper and piñon trees are also scattered throughout the area. Small animals, especially rabbits, desert rodents, and reptiles, are quite numerous. In the mountains that dot the Southwest, larger animals such as deer, antelope, bear, and foxes can be found.

Native Americans were able to adapt to the desert by using their ingenuity. Indigenous peoples utilized the varied plant and animal life that had adapted to the desert for their food. They also made use of plants, roots, stone, and wood to craft household utensils and tools.

Researchers today divide the prehistoric epoch of the southwestern Indians into several distinct periods, each of which is marked by specific cultural developments. Major eras in the Southwest include the *Desert Tradition*, which began approximately ten thousand years ago and lasted until 300 B.C.; the *Mogollon Tradition*, which endured from 300 B.C. to A.D. 1100; and the *Anasazi Tradition*, which began in A.D. 1100 and ended in the fourteenth century.

The culture of the earliest peoples in the Southwest is called the Desert Tradition. Sites inhabited by Desert people have been discovered at Concho in present-day eastern Arizona and at Bat Cave and Tularosa Cave in northern and central New Mexico.

Desert people depended on wild plants and animals for their food supply. In addition to the flora and fauna familiar to us today, several species of large animals roamed throughout the region thousands of years ago. Some of these animals, such as elephants and great bison, have become extinct in North America but were numerous in prehistoric times. They were hunted by Native peoples to provide food as well as hides used for clothing and shelter.

In addition to hunting large and small animals, Desert people created a method for preparing and cooking plant foods. They had many kinds of grinding stones, called *metates*, for grinding seeds and nuts.

Because they depended on natural resources for their survival, Desert people did not have permanent settlements. Instead, they shifted their camps from time to time in order to gather wild plants and to hunt migrating animals. Camps were fairly small, consisting of no more than a few families. Populations had to be limited due to the scarcity of permanent sources of food.

Desert people continued their foraging way of life for many thousands of years. Then, approximately five thousand years ago, they learned how to grow some of their own food. Corncobs have been discovered in prehistoric Desert sites dating from that time. Presumably, Desert people learned the art of agriculture from Native peoples in Mexico. Farming technology gradually spread from central Mexico northward into the Southwest through a process called cultural diffusion—the borrowing of skills by one group from a neighboring group.

For two thousand years after the beginnings of farming in Desert societies, corn was the only crop grown. Then, about three thousand years ago, Native peoples added new crops, especially varieties of beans and squash. Corn, beans, and squash have since remained the staple foods of southwestern peoples, including the modern Pueblo Indians.

Despite the incorporation of farming into their economies, Desert people did not abandon their previous way of life. They still lived in small groups and did not settle permanently in a fixed location. They also continued to hunt animals in the desert and mountains and to gather wild plants, nuts, and roots.

In 300 B.C., a profound change in Native culture took place. A new culture, or tradition, called Mogollon, developed. Mogollon people constructed permanent villages. They built rectangular or circular houses made of clay and stone. The Mogollon clustered houses together in small settlements so that approximately one hundred people lived in a typical Mogollon village, such as those found at Forestdale and Black River in Arizona and at Cibola and Mimbres in New Mexico.

Mogollon people also added several very important innovations to the existing stock of equipment. Perhaps of greatest significance, they began to make earthen pottery. Pots, bowls, and jars of various sizes and shapes were used for cooking, carrying, and storing foods and other supplies. Mogollon people fashioned many types of grinding stones, mortars, and pestles for preparing plant foods. They also began to use bows and arrows for hunting. Tools, utensils, and weapons were made from stone, bone, wood, and shell.

The next period of cultural change began about A.D. 1100. This new tradition was called the Anasazi. Anasazi people inhabited a large area, covering present-day New Mexico, most of Arizona, and the southern portions of Utah and Colorado. The largest Anasazi villages were concentrated in the region known today as the Four Corners, the area around the point where the borders of Arizona, New Mexico, Utah, and Colorado meet. Typical Anasazi settlements include Canyon de Chelly and Kayenta in Arizona, Mesa Verde in Colorado, and Chaco Canyon in New Mexico. (For additional information on these ancestors of the Hopis, enter "Anasazi" into any search engine and browse the many sites listed.)

Anasazi villages consisted of numerous rectangular houses, built of one, two, or three stories. Houses were adjacent to each other, forming rows of dwellings lined along streets. Towns also had open courtyards or plazas amidst the houses. Anasazi villages were much larger than settlements in previous periods, having populations of one thousand or more. Some of the largest sites, such as Point of Pines in northern Arizona, were inhabited by between two thousand and three thousand people in the fourteenth century.

Keet Seel, a grouping of cliff dwellings in northeastern Arizona, which is now part of Navajo National Monument, was home to the Hopis' ancestors, the Anasazi. who lived there from approximately A.D. 1250 to 1300.

The Anasazi utilized two different sources of water for their farmlands. They made use of floodwater by planting their crops near streams that overflowed during heavy rainstorms, and they diverted water from streams, channeling it into their fields.

Sometime in the fourteenth century, large Anasazi villages were suddenly abandoned. Most researchers today suggest that drastic climatic changes account for the movement of people to other locations and for the decrease in the size of towns. As the climate became more arid, sources of water diminished. Native peoples were forced to leave their villages to resettle in other areas. From that time on, different groups of Indians in the Southwest became culturally distinct. They are each identified by their own names, such as the Hopi, Zuñi, Tewa, Keres, and Towa. Some groups moved along the Rio Grande in what is now New Mexico and established villages there. They used the river's waters to irrigate their farms. Other people, including the Hopis, remained in desert lands in present-day northeastern Arizona. Although these people stayed in their traditional territory, they shifted the location of some of their settlements in order to adjust the population size to the available resources.

By the middle of the fourteenth century, these Hopi settlements underwent some dramatic changes. Until that time, the Hopis had lived either in small villages or on isolated farmsteads. They were concentrated in northern Arizona, near Kayenta and Black Mesa. But during the hundred years from about 1350 to 1450, the Hopis abandoned Kayenta because of climatic changes and drought. Hopi villages farther south grew rapidly in size as more Hopis relocated there. Hopi villages were located at or near their present-day sites south of Black Mesa in an area approximately sixty miles wide. Villages were typically inhabited by between five hundred and one thousand people.

The location of Hopi settlements was advantageous for farming. Since they were situated south of Black Mesa, strong winds blew sand from the mesa onto Hopi territory, forming sand dunes that retained moisture. The Hopis then planted their crops near the dunes, benefiting from the moisture in the soil. They built windbreaks of brush and stone to keep the high winds from damaging their crops.

Over the centuries, the Hopis had skillfully developed strains of corn and beans that were adapted to dry conditions. The plants had very long roots, sometimes fifteen to twenty feet in length. These roots secured the plants in the ground and enabled them to withstand strong gusts of wind. Long roots also made it possible for plants to absorb whatever moisture lay deep within the soil.

In the fourteenth century, the Hopis invented a new style of pottery. Although all Pueblo peoples made pottery, Hopi decorative styles changed considerably. In previous centuries, pottery was painted with black-on-white geometric designs. But Hopi women began to use black-on-orange, black-on-yellow, and multicolor decorations. Their innovative designs testify to an explosion of artistic imagination and skill. In addition to the geometric forms, they painted sweeping curved lines and naturalistic figures. Subject matter included various animals, birds, flowers, and human beings. Both individual figures and group scenes were depicted.

Hopi artists also painted dramatic murals on walls of buildings that they used for conducting ceremonies. The multicolor paintings showed scenes of animals, humans, and mythological figures. They were used during rituals to represent characters and events in myths. After a ceremony ended, the murals were washed over with a coating of plain plaster. When the Hopis performed another ceremony, a new mural was painted on the wall. Modern researchers at a Hopi settlement called Awatovi have recently found walls with a hundred layers of plaster. Of these, thirty layers contained paintings.

Coal mining was another cultural development unique to the Hopis. In the fourteenth century, they began to mine coal found near their villages. Hopis most often used the technique of strip-mining. They removed surface soil and dug out the coal situated underneath. Their tools included picks, scrapers, and hammer stones. The Hopis extracted coal that lay deeper beneath the surface by constructing underground mines. Researchers today estimate that some Hopi communities in the fourteenth through sixteenth centuries extracted as much as 450 pounds of coal each day. Approximately thirty thousand tons were mined by residents of Awatovi during a period that lasted three centuries.

The Hopis employed coal for many purposes, including cooking, heating, firing pottery, and pigmenting ceramics and paintings. They saved the ash from coal fires and used it as a bed for flagstones that formed the floors of their houses. The Hopis also constructed stoves with chimneys, apparently in reaction to the noxious smoke made by burning coal.

In sum, Hopi culture contained many features common to all the Pueblos. They lived in houses and villages built on a Pueblo model and grew crops common throughout the region. But the Hopis also developed unique traits, using their own skills, inventions, and artistic imagination.

Pueblo tribes like the Hopi remained in the Southwest into the historic period—that is, the sixteenth century. Although the Spanish who arrived in the area in the sixteenth century referred to all the Natives by the same term, the Pueblos had distinct cultures and spoke different languages. They also lived in numerous villages throughout the region. Native peoples who resided in villages along the Rio Grande in New Mexico called themselves by names that included Tewa, Towa, Tano, and Keres. Farther to the west, the Hopis and other tribes such as the Zuñis made their homes.

Languages spoken by the Pueblos are quite diverse. Several completely different language families are represented. The Hopi language belongs to a family called Uto-Aztecan, distantly related to the language spoken by the Aztecs in Mexico. The language of the nearby Zuñis is not related to Hopi. Linguists today are uncertain as to whether Zuñi is a "language isolate" with no known connections or whether it belongs to a family called Penutian. If Zuñi is a Penutian language, it is a remote relative of languages spoken in parts of California. Pueblo living in towns along the Rio Grande speak languages belonging to two other families, called Tanoan and Keresan.

In addition to the Pueblos, other Indian tribes lived in the Southwest. Some of these groups were on friendly terms with the Hopis and traded with them. Farming peoples such as the Pimas, Papagos, and Havasupais inhabited parts of western Arizona. Contact between them and the Hopis was intermittent but generally peaceful.

Other groups in the region had a very different way of life. The Utes from present-day Utah and the Navajos who lived in what is now Arizona and New Mexico occasionally supplemented their own economies by raiding sedentary Hopi villages. They took crops, turkeys, and other goods from the fields and towns. In these raids, people on both sides were sometimes killed. But despite occasional conflict, the Hopis also traded with the Utes and the Navajos.

Through the centuries, the Hopis considered themselves safe and secure in their ancient homeland. They had a rich cultural history on which to build their future.

3

The
Hopi
World

The Hopis live on land that is beautiful and majestic. Yet they also live in an environment that presents enormous problems for people pursuing a way of life dependent on farming. The Southwest region is extremely arid. There are a few permanent springs in the area from which people can get drinking water, but these springs do not supply enough water to irrigate fields. No permanent rivers or streams flow in Hopi territory.

In this context, the Hopis are forced to depend on rain as the only source of water for their farmlands. But rain cannot provide security. Annual rainfall is relatively slight, averaging only ten inches per year. In some years, there is not enough rain and then crops dry out and die. In other years, summer rains come in sudden torrential downpours that drown the young and growing plants. The people hope for good years of balanced rainfall, sufficient but not excessive.

The growing season itself is relatively short. Even though spring and summer days are sunny and warm, the high altitude of Hopi land results in sharp differences in temperature between day and night. At altitudes of six thousand feet, night-time frosts come early in the fall and harm immature plants.

Because resources are uncertain, villages are relatively small, with most towns having around five hundred residents. Populations have to be small in order to keep within the limits of farming in a desert environment.

Hopi villages are permanent, having maintained their locations for at least seven hundred years. Before the arrival of the Spanish, there were six main town sites and perhaps a few smaller ones dispersed throughout the territory. The major towns were called *Walpi* (WAL-pi; "place of the ravine"), *Awatovi* (a-WA-to-bi; "high place of the bow"), *Oraibi* (o-RAY-bi; "gray-rock place"), *Mishongnovi* (mi-SHONG-no-vi; "large boulder"), *Shongopavi* (shong-GO-pa-vi; "sand-grass spring place"), and *Shipaulovi* (shi-POW-lo-vi; "place of mosquitoes").

All Hopi villages are built on the same plan. They consist of clay and stone houses that are placed next to each other along rows forming streets. Houses contain from one to several square rooms and may be one, two, or three stories high.

Villages also have one or more kivas in which rituals are performed. In addition, each village contains at least one large open courtyard or plaza where people gather and hold public dances and rituals. Houses line the plazas, providing places from which people can view communal events.

Families who live together in a house are related through a system of kinship that anthropologists call a *lineage*. A lineage is a group of people who claim descent from a common ancestor. Hopi lineages follow lines of descent through women. This is what anthropologists call a *matrilineal system*, a term meaning "mother's line."

Households typically consist of an elder woman, her husband, their daughters, and their unmarried sons. When a

Mishongnovi was one of six major Hopi towns that existed at the time the Spanish arrived in the sixteenth century. A typical Hopi village consisted of clay and stone houses that were placed next to each other along rows forming streets.

man marries, he goes to live with his wife's family. Married women remain with their own families. A large number of people may reside together in one house, helping each other with family tasks and looking after each other's children.

The senior woman in a household has great influence over other members. She gives advice about family matters and plans and coordinates joint activities. Her eldest daughter also has much influence in the household. She assumes her mother's duties when the elder woman is away from home and will succeed to the position of household leader after the mother's death.

Although men move to their wives' homes, they maintain strong ties to their parents and relatives. A man visits his kin frequently. He takes part in family events and may serve as a disciplinarian to his sisters' children. Hopi men often consider the households of their mothers and sisters to be their real homes.

The senior woman of each lineage sets aside a room in her house for the storage of ceremonial objects. Items such as masks, tobacco pipes, religious figurines, rattles, and feathers are kept there. The most important ritual object safeguarded in the room is a sacred ear of corn that symbolizes the lineage and its members. The corn is carefully wrapped in cloth and feathers and kept on a specially erected altar.

The Hopi system of kinship also contains units called clans. A clan is a grouping of people who consider themselves to be related, although they may not be able to trace their actual relationship to one another. A clan may consist of hundreds of people. It is different from a lineage, which typically contains a smaller number of known relatives in a direct line of descent. Just as Hopi lineages are based on descent through women, membership in clans also follows matrilineal principles. A child automatically belongs to his or her mother's clan.

Hopi clans are named after animals, birds, foods, natural substances, and objects. For example, some clans have bird names: Sparrow, Hawk, Parrot, Dove, Eagle, and Bluebird; others are named after mammals, reptiles, or insects: Badger, Bear, Coyote, Snake, Lizard, and Butterfly; some have the names of foods: Corn and Squash; and others are named for various plants and substances: Sand, Fog, Snow, Reed, and Cactus. (For additional information on these family groups, enter "Hopi clans" into any search engine and browse the many sites listed.)

One of the older women in each clan is designated as the head of the clan. She is called the clan mother. Clan mothers make decisions regarding members of their clan, help settle disputes among them, and give advice about family matters. When the head of a clan dies, the next oldest woman in the group usually succeeds to her position.

The brother of a clan mother also has a prominent place in clan activities, and his opinions and advice carry much weight. He also plays an important role in organizing and conducting family ceremonies.

People within each clan follow certain rules of behavior. First of all, they are not permitted to marry members of their own clan. A child's mother and father must therefore be members of different groups. The Hopis also believe that one should not marry a member of one's father's clan. Violating this rule is not as serious as marrying within one's own group but it is nonetheless considered improper and is rarely done.

Clan members help each other in times of crisis. If someone's crops have failed, or if someone is ill or in distress, clan mates are expected to lend economic or emotional support and comfort. Although the Hopis believe that all people should be kind, generous, and helpful to others, clan mates should be especially so.

In addition to their social functions, clans are landholding units. Hopi land is not owned by individuals but rather by clans. Each clan has its specific territory, marked by boundary stones at the corners. The stones are painted with symbols representing the group. Clan mothers divide clan land among the women who are heads of lineages. These women then assign portions of the land to their daughters and their daughters' families.

Each family is given access to farmland in several locations. Since the Hopis live in a climate where there are extremes of rainfall and temperature, they can never be certain that plants will necessarily grow. For example, some land may be on higher or lower ground and some may be closer or farther from streams or places where runoff from summer rains tends to accumulate. Because of this uncertainty, it is essential for Hopi farmers to distribute their crops in a number of locations, hoping that at least some of them will fare well. It is for this same reason that the head of a household gives her daughters sections of farmland in various areas under her control.

Before the arrival of Europeans in North America, the Hopis followed a division of labor based on gender—that is, men and women were assigned different economic tasks. Men were the farmers. They prepared fields, planted and tended crops, and harvested them in the summer and fall. Before a man married, he helped his father farm the land given to his mother. After marriage, a man worked on the land under his wife's control.

Hopi farmers grew various crops to support themselves and their families. Several types of corn were the staples of the diet, including white, blue, and sweet corn. Numerous varieties of beans and squash supplemented corn dishes. The planting season began in April when men planted the first crop of corn. This batch was ready for harvest in mid-July, in time for the kachina Niman ceremony. In May, men planted more corn, along with beans and squash. Men in former times also planted tobacco and cotton. They wove cotton into cloth and then fashioned clothing, blankets, and sashes for their families. The harvest period lasted from late summer through autumn, depending on the growing season for each variety of plant.

In addition to farming, men hunted near their villages for small animals such as rabbits and other desert rodents. They occasionally traveled farther into the mountains surrounding Hopi territory to hunt antelope and deer.

Men made the tools they used for farming and hunting. Farm implements were fairly simple, for the most part consisting of digging sticks, wooden shovels, and stone axes. Hunting gear included wooden bows and arrows tipped with stone arrowheads. Men also made the weapons and shields that they used in warfare, and they wove the baskets used for carrying or storing food and equipment. Other necessary tasks that men performed included cutting and hauling the firewood

Farming has traditionally been undertaken by Hopi men, who raised such crops as corn, squash, and beans. Here, a farmer stands in his rainwater-only irrigated cornfield on the Hopi Reservation in northeastern Arizona.

used for cooking and for heating houses during the very cold winters. Finally, crafting beautiful jewelry from stones of turquoise, shell, and coral was also a male occupation.

Hopi women were responsible for work within the household. They prepared corn for cooking by shelling corn kernels and grinding them into a fine meal. Each household owned three grinding stones called metates that were kept in a large wooden frame when not in use. The stones were distinguished by the thickness of their edges, and each produced cornmeal of different degrees of coarseness. They could be used in succession to make the finest powder.

Households also owned a cooking stone called a *piki* stone that women used to make piki, which remains one of the

Hopis' most prized foods even today. Piki is a wafer-thin bread made of fine blue cornmeal. Women begin by building a fire under the piki stone and spreading cottonseed oil on its surface. Then they spread a thin batter of cornmeal on the hot stone. When the bread is cooked, the woman peels it off and rolls it or folds it for serving. Piki is eaten at daily meals as well as on ceremonial occasions.

Other dishes of corn breads and hominy were eaten regularly. In addition, Hopi women prepared several varieties of beans. When beans were harvested, they were dried and stored for later use. When the Hopis were ready to eat them, they boiled and roasted the dried beans. Meals often included different types of squash. Women also boiled or roasted meat when it was available. Some meat was supplied by the efforts of men who hunted the animals, but the Hopis also traditionally kept large flocks of turkeys that they used for food.

Women made pottery, including bowls used for cooking and serving food. They crafted many different kinds of earthen containers used for storing corn and other essential items.

Finally, women had primary responsibility for caring for their children as well as for general household tasks. They periodically plastered the walls in their houses with fresh layers of mud to keep the walls unbroken and the rooms clean.

Relationships between Hopi women and men were based on a philosophy of balance and reciprocity. Men and women learned different skills and performed different tasks, but they were considered equally important and valuable. Men depended on women for the work they did, and women depended on men's labor as well; both men and women contributed to their family's survival.

The Hopis made extensive use of many varieties of wild plants. Some of these were eaten, some were used as medicines, and others had household or personal purposes. For example, roots of the yucca plant produce a soapy substance that is used for washing hair. Hair washing was not only part of personal hygiene but was also an important feature of many rituals, including ceremonies marking the naming of babies, girls' puberty rites, and marriages.

In traditional times, men wore woven cotton shirts and aprons over deerskin leggings. Women wore woven blouses and skirts. Clothing was sometimes brightly embroidered with contrasting colors and designs. Both women and men adorned themselves with sashes, necklaces, and articles of turquoise and shell jewelry. To protect their feet, they wore moccasins and boots made of deer or antelope hide.

Scenes of life in Hopi villages can be summed up by the words of Antonio de Espejo, leader of a Spanish expedition through Pueblo territory in 1582:

> As we crossed this province the inhabitants of each town came out to meet us, took us to their pueblos, and gave us quantities of turkeys, corn, beans, and tortillas, with other kinds of bread which they make skillfully. . . . They grind raw corn on very large stones, five or six women working together, and from the flour they make many kinds of bread. Their houses are two, three, or four stories high, each house being partitioned into a number of rooms. In this province, some of the Natives are clad in cotton blankets or dressed deer skins. The women have cotton skirts, often embroidered with colored thread, and over their shoulders a blanket fastened at the waist by a strip of embroidered material, with tassels. The women arrange their hair neatly and prettily.

Young Hopi women fashioned their hair into a distinctive style when they reached puberty. They parted their hair in the middle and formed each half into a tight pinwheel on either side of their head above the ear. Young women adopted this hairstyle after puberty but abandoned it when they married.

Hopi marriages were marked by ceremonial exchanges of gifts between a prospective bride and groom. Before her wedding, a bride-to-be spent four days in her mother-in-law's household, grinding cornmeal and making piki bread. This bread became the feast meal served at the wedding. During the same period, male relatives of the groom went to a kiva where they spun cotton into cloth and made wedding clothes for the bride. The men were later thanked by the bride and her female relatives with gifts of piki.

The exchange of gifts at marriages symbolically expressed the balance and reciprocity of women's and men's work. By giving piki bread to their mothers-in-law, brides offered food that was typically produced by women. And by giving clothing to the bride, male relatives of the groom offered products normally made by men.

Throughout Hopi history, family life has emphasized the ideals of harmony and cooperation among members. People are expected to help one another, to be generous in sharing what they have, and to treat each other with kindness and respect. The Hopis like people who are even-tempered and refrain from showing anger or engaging in arguments.

Children are taught these values by the example and words of their elders. A young child is showered with affection and attention. The child is liberally indulged by all adults during its first two years of life. But when a child reaches the age of two, an age distinguished by the ability to walk, parental attitudes begin to change. The child is then considered to be responsible for his or her actions. Adults teach children the norms of proper behavior and the values of Hopi life. Children are also trained to endure discomfort or displeasure without complaining.

Children who misbehave are admonished by their parents and other family members. They may be sternly lectured by their mother's brother when he returns home for visits. In addition, adults may threaten children by telling them that ogres or giants will come and whip them or carry them away. Indeed, from time to time, two men dressed in special clothing and frightening masks walk through the village and act as disciplinarians. When parents see these men approach their house, they tell their children to hide so that they will not be caught. But if a child misbehaves often, his or her parents may arrange in advance for the disciplinarians to come to the house, find the child, and give the girl or boy a forceful scolding or a light whipping.

Since Hopi villages are relatively small, it is not necessary to have an extensive set of political officials to govern the town. Each village, though, has a town chief, called *kikmongwi* (kik-MON-wee), a title meaning "leader of the house." While a kikmongwi gives advice and has influence over others, these chiefs have no absolute power to enforce decisions. It is not surprising that in a society in which everything is understood within a religious context, the kikmongwi's most important functions are ritual; that they supervise the planning and preparation of village ceremonies is considered much more important than any political role they play.

Town chiefs are selected by a village council made up of leaders of all the clans represented in the village. Clan leaders also serve as advisors and assistants to the town chief. A town chief must be a man belonging to the Bear clan. Other qualifications include such character traits as intelligence, even-temperedness, kindness, and generosity. He should be a good farmer and a reliable and cooperative member of his family and community. In the words of Leslie White, an anthropologist and observer of Hopi life, a town chief behaves as follows: "The chief should hold himself somewhat aloof from the daily and mundane affairs of the [village]; he is supposed to concentrate on spiritual affairs. He should take no part in any quarrels. Everyone should treat him with kindness and respect. And the chief should have only kindly feelings toward his people."

A town chief holds his position for life. However, if he becomes arrogant or abuses his rights, or if he shows himself to be incompetent, he can be removed from office by the village council of clan leaders.

Each town chief has a special assistant called the town crier. This man has the duty of making public announcements on behalf of the chief or at the request of heads of the various ritual associations. The crier climbs to the rooftop of one of the central houses in the village and makes his announcement for all to hear. Messages usually relate to the timing of events such as the beginning of the planting season or upcoming community ceremonies.

Each Hopi village is considered a separate political entity. There is no formal structure uniting the towns into any sort of larger unit. Decisions are made within each village and affect only residents of that town.

The Hopis have no system of formal laws dictating how people should behave or setting punishments for wrongdoers. But an individual's actions come under the collective scrutiny of family and neighbors. People who wrong others may be reprimanded by the head of their household or lineage. They may also become targets of gossip and be teased about their actions by anyone in the community. When people meet with such public criticism, they usually correct their behavior and try to avoid any further slights to others.

The Hopis believe that people who commit wrongful acts or think bad thoughts may become ill. In keeping with their philosophy of harmony and balance, the Hopis think that disease can come from disturbing an individual's internal peace. People maintain internal harmony by having a good heart, and a good heart is reflected in good deeds and kind thoughts.

When a Hopi becomes ill, she or he can seek a cure from healers who use a variety of therapies. Some treatments rely on the medicinal properties of natural substances contained in plants and roots. Hopi women and men who are healers know how to make therapeutic teas from numerous wild plants. Patients drink the teas as part of their cure. Healers may also treat illnesses by performing rituals intended to correct imbalances within a patient's heart or mind. Through prayers and appeals to spirits, a patient's good heart can be restored.

The Hopis' way of life helped keep their communities together in peace and harmony for many centuries. Although the Hopis sometimes encountered dangers from environmental conditions such as droughts and from occasional raids by enemies, they were able to survive and maintain their culture. Then, in the sixteenth century, a group of foreign intruders arrived in Hopi territory. These invaders from Spain set off a series of events that brought unforeseen problems to the Hopis and their neighbors. However, despite the onslaught, first by Spanish and later by U.S. forces, the Hopis have been remarkably successful at withstanding foreign domination. Even though they have modified their culture somewhat, they have largely kept to their ancient values and traditions.

4

Facing the Intruders

The first European intruders into Pueblo territory were Spanish soldiers and missionaries who ventured north from their bases in Mexico in the early sixteenth century. After they had defeated and plundered the rich Aztec Empire in central Mexico, Spanish officials began to look elsewhere for new lands and new peoples to draw into their domain.

In 1539, a Franciscan priest named Marcos de Niza traveled into present-day New Mexico and Arizona. From a distance, he spotted the village of the Zuñis. He did not actually visit the Zuñis or any other Pueblo settlement but instead returned to Mexico and told fantastic tales of rich cities, golden treasures, and great wealth to be found in these lands to the north. When Spanish officials heard the stories, they organized expeditions to explore the region.

The first contingent was led by Francisco Vásquez de Coronado in 1540. He journeyed into Pueblo territory with a large company

Francisco Vásquez de Coronado led the first wave of Spanish explorers into Hopi territory in the mid-1500s. The Hopis learned not to trust the newcomers when Coronado ordered the execution of several hundred residents of the town of Tiguex. The residents had tried to expel the Spaniards because of their unquenchable need for Hopi goods.

of several hundred soldiers on foot and on horseback. Among the Spanish travelers were a number of priests belonging to the Franciscan order of the Roman Catholic Church. They wanted to establish missions in Indian communities and convert the Native peoples to Christianity.

Coronado set up headquarters in a Hopi pueblo called Tiguex near present-day Bernadillo, New Mexico. He remained there for two years. During that time, Coronado sent expeditions to visit other pueblos along the Rio Grande and also sent explorers to the Hopis' western settlements. Pedro de Tovar led a group of twenty soldiers and one Catholic priest to make contact with residents of the prominent Hopi village of Awatovi.

At first, the Natives welcomed the Spaniards. They traded with the newcomers and obtained metal tools and utensils from them. The Spanish were given food and clothing by the Pueblos. But Spaniards began to demand more and more goods from the people. The residents of Tiguex soon resented the Spaniards' demands and tried to expel them from the village. The revolt was unsuccessful because the Pueblos' bows and arrows were no match for the Spaniards' guns. Not content with simply putting down the Native uprising, Coronado ordered several hundred Tiguex residents to be executed in retaliation for the uprising. The example of Spanish brutality against defenseless people was quickly told among all the Pueblos. Thereafter, the Pueblos no longer looked upon the Spanish as friendly visitors but as potential threats.

The Pueblos' worst fears about Spanish intentions came to pass throughout the sixteenth and seventeenth centuries. Although the Pueblo Indians in the eastern villages along the Rio Grande suffered the most at the hands of the Spanish, the Hopis, too, were burdened by Spanish demands for goods and labor. To force the Hopis to do their will, the Spanish lashed them with whips and brutally killed them in summary executions.

A number of expeditions were sent from Mexico to make further inroads into Pueblo territory. In 1582, Antonio de Espejo led a large group of soldiers and missionaries into the region. They traveled throughout the area, visiting Hopi villages in the west and other pueblos in the east. Judging from the Spaniards' own accounts, it seems that Espejo and his men were just as cruel as Coronado had been. For example, one of Espejo's companions, Diego Pérez de Luxán, described an incident that occurred in a town when the Spanish entered and demanded food and other provisions. Since the residents had heard about the Spanish from other Pueblo people, they refused the foreigners' requests. In response, according to Luxán: "the corners of the pueblo were taken by four men, and four others began to seize those natives who showed themselves. And as the pueblo was large and the majority had hidden themselves, we set fire to the big pueblo, where we thought some were burned to death because of the cries they uttered. We at once took out prisoners, two at a time, and lined them up, where they were shot many times until they were dead. Sixteen were executed, not counting those who burned to death."

In the late sixteenth century, the Spanish government embarked on a new policy. Instead of simply sending expeditions to explore Pueblo territory, they decided to establish permanent colonies of Spanish settlers in the region. Juan de Oñate led the first group of colonizers into New Mexico in 1598. There, Oñate set up his base at a Pueblo village, demanding provisions from the inhabitants. Oñate's methods were similar to those employed by Coronado and Espejo. According to accounts written by one of his associates, Oñate "sent people out every month in various directions to bring maize [corn] from the pueblos. The feelings of the natives against supplying it cannot be exaggerated for they weep and cry out as if they were being killed. The Spaniards seize the blankets by force, leaving the poor Indians stark naked."

Even Spanish authorities in Mexico considered Oñate's activities outrageous. They removed him as governor of the colony in 1607 and appointed a replacement, Pedro de Peralta. Peralta arrived in 1609 and shifted the Spanish headquarters to the pueblo of Santa Fe, which remained the provincial capital throughout the Spanish colonial period.

Unfortunately, Peralta turned out to be no different from his predecessors. He began by forcing the Pueblos in Santa Fe to build a palace and other public buildings for his government to use. The Spanish also compelled Native Americans throughout the province to give them food, blankets, and other goods as tribute. Some Pueblos were enslaved and made to work on farms or in mines and workshops owned by Spaniards; others were forced to serve the Spaniards as domestic servants.

Franciscan missionaries were no better than government authorities or soldiers in their dealings with the Pueblos. They, too, established large farms and forced the Natives to work for them in their fields and homes. Indeed, missionaries often held huge amounts of land that produced much more food than was necessary to subsist. They sold the surplus to Spanish officials, soldiers, and settlers and received large profits from this business.

Priests established missions in many Pueblo communities, forcing the residents to erect churches and housing for the missionaries. They ordered all the inhabitants to attend church services and to abandon their traditional religious practices. They also destroyed Pueblo ritual objects and religious works of art.

The Franciscans dealt harshly with the Pueblos, who resisted their attempts to impose the Catholic religion on Native American societies. They meted out public whippings, torture, and even executions as punishments for Pueblo Indians who continued to perform their own ancient rituals.

In 1629, three Franciscans journeyed to Hopi villages and established their first mission at Awatovi, headed by Francisco Porras. Although Porras wanted to convert the Hopis and also demanded their provisions and labor, he was less cruel in his methods than many other missionaries and officials had been. Porras was actually somewhat sympathetic toward Hopi people and their culture. For example, he learned to speak the Hopi language in an attempt to communicate directly with them. This was unusual, as most priests spoke only Spanish and used bilingual Natives as interpreters. In fact, the heads of Franciscan orders in Mexico and Spain ordered the priests not to learn Indian languages because they were worried that if missionaries spoke directly with the Native peoples, they might sympathize with the Indians' complaints against Spanish authorities.

In addition to the mission at Awatovi, churches were built in the Hopi villages of Oraibi and Shongopavi. Smaller visitation sites were established in several other towns.

Once a major Hopi town, Oraibi was one of the first locations where the Franciscans established a Catholic church. However, the Hopis largely resisted the Spaniards' attempt to convert them to Catholicism.

At Awatovi, Porras had some minimal success in converting some of the inhabitants to Catholicism. The Hopis elsewhere showed no interest in the new religion, and even at Awatovi, Catholic adherents were in the minority.

However, the Franciscans did have far-reaching effects on Hopi life. They introduced the Hopis to many articles of European manufacture. The Hopis especially prized European tools and utensils made of metal, including knives, axes, saws, scissors, and nails. Hopi farmers also began to plant some crops obtained from the Spanish, such as peaches, apples, melons, tomatoes, and chilies. The latter two foods had originated among the Aztecs in Mexico but were adopted by Spaniards and taken with them into what is now the

American Southwest. Finally, the Hopis added sheep and cattle to their livestock.

By the middle of the seventeenth century, a series of recurring disasters affected Hopi communities. Severe droughts occurred in the 1640s and 1660s, resulting in crop failures and food shortages. In addition, raids by neighboring Navajo people increased during the same period. The Navajos were no doubt affected by the same drought and lost much of their own produce. They therefore turned to raiding Hopi villages in an attempt to obtain the food and goods they needed for their own survival.

Waves of epidemic diseases such as smallpox and measles struck Hopi settlements in the middle of the seventeenth century. These diseases were previously unknown among the Hopis, indeed among all Native American communities. Just as particular plants and animals are indigenous to certain areas of the world, organisms that cause diseases also originate in specific regions. Germs that cause smallpox and measles were found in Europe but were absent from North and South America before the arrival of Europeans on these continents. Since Native Americans had never been exposed to smallpox and measles, they had not developed any natural immunity or resistance to the diseases. The result was that when the Hopis and other Natives first encountered the germs, they succumbed to the diseases in enormous numbers. In some cases, all the members of a household died in the epidemics. Few, if any, families were left untouched.

The combination of droughts, raids, and epidemics severely undermined the stability of Hopi society in the seventeenth century. Many Hopis sought the cause of their misfortunes and found it in the Spanish. The Hopis believed that the balance and harmony of their universe had been disturbed by the foreigners' arrival. Seen from the Hopis' point of view, the Spanish not only had demanded crops, goods, and labor from them but had also overturned the delicate relationships between humans and the natural world that are vital to life and happiness. By attempting to destroy the Hopi religion, missionaries had violated sacred bonds between the Hopis, their ancestors, and their spiritual protectors.

The Hopis often reacted to Spanish abuses by outwardly conforming to their demands. They knew that resistance was futile and would result in brutal retaliation. Sometimes, though, actions by local Spaniards were too outrageous to be ignored. For instance, in 1655, a Hopi delegation traveled to Santa Fe to lodge a complaint with the Spanish governor against a priest in one of their villages who had arrested a leader of a Hopi ritual society. The priest had the man whipped, doused with hot oil, and set on fire. Spanish officials listened to the charges but, as usual, took no steps to punish the priest nor to end the repeated abuses.

After living under Spanish control for more than a century and a half, the Pueblo people finally could endure no more demands and outrages. In 1680, Pueblo leaders began to meet together in secret to devise a plan to rid themselves of the intruders. Most prominent among the leaders was a man named Pope (Po-PAY), a member of a Pueblo tribe known as the Tewa. Pope was from the village of San Juan, located near the Rio Grande in New Mexico, and had himself been a victim of Spanish cruelty in 1675, being one of a group of ritual leaders publicly whipped by Spanish authorities for allegedly engaging in witchcraft.

Pope and leaders from all of the Pueblo tribes decided to stage a rebellion against the Spanish in an effort to drive them from the region. After many meetings, the leaders decided on a plan of action that would begin by laying siege to the provincial headquarters in Santa Fe. They wanted to time their attack to occur during the summer of 1680, because they knew that the Spanish would be awaiting new shipments of goods from Mexico, and therefore their supply of guns and ammunition would be low. Pope and the others thought the Spanish would surrender and leave the area if they realized they were cut off from receiving additional food and provisions.

In addition to the siege of Santa Fe, the plan called for participation by all Pueblo communities. Leaders agreed that residents of all the pueblos would attack the Spanish officials, soldiers, and priests who resided in their villages. They set August 11, 1680, as the date for the uprising. Two messengers were chosen to relay the final plan to each pueblo. However, by some means, the Spanish governor, Antonio de Otermin, found out about the impending revolt. On August 9, he arrested the two messengers. When word of the arrests spread in the pueblos, Pope and the other leaders decided to implement their plan immediately. The *Pueblo Revolt*, as it is called, began on August 10. The most concerted attacks occurred in villages along the Rio Grande. The rebels successfully cut off water and supplies to Santa Fe and routed nearby Spanish settlers. Soldiers and priests were killed. Otermin finally realized that his forces were unable to defeat the Pueblos and ordered a retreat from Santa Fe on August 21. (For additional information on this Native uprising, enter "Pueblo Revolt of 1680" into any search engine and browse the many sites listed.)

Although the Hopis lived far from the New Mexican villages, they, too, participated in the rebellion. They killed the five priests living in their villages and destroyed the churches they had previously been forced to build.

Once Spanish settlers, priests, and soldiers began to retreat from Pueblo territory, the Natives ceased their attacks. They allowed the foreigners to depart without further incident. Pueblo behavior was thus vastly different from the brutal retaliations that Spanish authorities had often meted out to the Native nations.

Peace lasted for only twelve years. In 1692, Diego de Vargas led an army back to Pueblo land and successfully imposed control over most of the villages. He and his soldiers executed hundreds of Pueblo resisters and defenseless villagers. Vargas visited Hopi settlements, planning to regain dominance there, too. But after the revolt of 1680, the Hopis had moved their villages from the open desert to the tops of three mesas located within their territory. Since the mesas were compact areas and had only one path leading to the top, the Hopis knew they could easily spot invaders and block their ascent to the villages.

The Hopis were correct. Vargas tried to attack them but failed to enter their towns. The Hopis were helped by groups of Navajos and Utes who raided the Spanish soldiers.

Spanish authorities sent additional expeditions into Hopi territory with the aim of either convincing the Hopis to submit to Spanish control or forcing them to do so. Both plans failed repeatedly, and Hopi communities successfully withstood foreign domination. They were aided by a number of immigrants from other Pueblo communities in New Mexico who sought refuge among the western Hopis. The largest group of refugees arrived from the Tewa pueblos in 1696. They took up permanent residence on First Mesa, the easternmost of the three Hopi mesas. The Tewa village, called Hano, shared First Mesa with the Hopi towns of Sichomovi and Walpi.

Franciscan priests made several more attempts to regain a foothold in Hopi towns during the 1690s. Only the residents of Awatovi allowed the priests to set up a mission in their town. All other Hopis were strongly opposed to the priests. They objected to the missionaries' efforts to convert them to Christianity, and they feared that former demands for labor and the brutal practices of the Spaniards would be forced upon them once again. After failing to convince the people at Awatovi to expel the Franciscans, the Hopis, led by a clan chief named Espeleta, attacked the village in 1701. They killed all the men and forced the women and children to leave the village. Later that year, the Spanish governor in Santa Fe sent an army against the Hopis to punish them for sacking the Catholic mission at Awatovi, but his soldiers were defeated by the Hopis.

Throughout the eighteenth century, Spanish authorities made occasional attempts to reimpose control over Hopi communities. Expeditions were sent in 1707, 1716, 1775, and 1780. The Hopis, however, were steadfast in their refusal to allow the Spaniards to enter their villages.

With the Pueblo Revolt of 1680, the Hopis had finally been able to rid themselves of Spanish domination. They were successful for several reasons. First, Hopi warriors used their military skills and planning to defend their communities. Second, since Hopi settlements were distant from the center of Spanish colonization in New Mexico, the expenses required for the Spanish to mount repeated campaigns against the Hopis proved excessive. Because of the expense, the Spanish could not maintain continual pressure against the Hopis. Third, the Navajos, Apaches, and Utes who lived in the area between the Hopis and the Spanish colonies attacked Spanish soldiers on their way to Hopi territory. Because of the Hopis' defensive strength and favorable external circumstances, they were able to safeguard their communities and maintain their culture in relative stability.

Freed from Spanish demands for produce and labor, the Hopis once again devoted their time to traditional pursuits and even experienced an economic recovery in the eighteenth century. As described by Silvestre Velez de Escalante, a Franciscan traveler to Hopi territory in 1775, the Hopi "are very civilized, apply themselves to weaving and cultivating the land by means of which they raise abundant crops of maize, beans, and chile. They also gather cotton."

Although the Hopi population had declined since the mid-1600s because of disease and warfare, by the middle of the eighteenth century, the size of Hopi communities had begun to increase again. In 1742, for instance, a Spanish visitor put the number of Hopis at 10,846. This figure probably represents a decline from their aboriginal population but was nonetheless an increase over the previous century.

Still, environmental and external conditions continued to adversely affect Hopi villages from time to time. Several years of severe drought set in beginning in 1777, which resulted in crop failures and famine. During the same period, the Hopis were the victims of Navajo raids. Because of these difficulties, approximately 150 Hopis decided to leave their towns and seek aid and relief from the Pueblos in New Mexico. Soon afterward, when the rains came and the crisis lessened, most of the refugees returned to their own villages.

Once again, the Hopis regained their economic stability. They lived according to their traditional way of life, honoring their ancestors and the spirit beings who they believed protected them. Free again to follow their ancient ideals of harmony and balance, the Hopis felt satisfied that they had stayed true to their own way of life.

5

Challenges to Harmony

The nineteenth century began for the Hopis as a time of economic and spiritual recovery. Because of their isolation from centers of colonial control, they were able to turn their energies to producing crops and maintaining their households. And they devoted their hearts and minds to honoring the spirit world. But as the century wore on, new intruders entered Hopi territory and challenged their stability and peace.

The Spanish colonies of New Mexico and Arizona came under the control of the Republic of Mexico when it gained its independence from Spain in 1821. Although Mexico had jurisdiction over its northern provinces from that year until the end of the Mexican-American War in 1848, the Pueblos living in New Mexico had little contact with government authorities. The Hopis in Arizona were totally ignored by the Mexicans.

Several factors contributed to the Hopis' continued isolation. First, their history of strong resistance to foreign domination led Mexican officials to leave them in peace. Second, the great distance between Hopi territory and centers of government in Mexico made contact costly in terms of time and money. Third, the Hopis' determination to resist efforts to have Christianity imposed on them meant that even the Franciscan priests did not make serious efforts to establish missions in Hopi villages. Finally, although tens of thousands of Hispanic settlers lived near the Rio Grande Pueblo in New Mexico, few of them ventured west into Hopi territory because they were fearful of raids by the Navajos and Apaches who lived in the western region.

The Mexican government changed the official legal status of Native Americans in the former Spanish colonies. Under Spain, the Hopis and other Native Americans had been considered wards of the Crown, but Mexico granted full citizenship to all Native peoples. Although the legal change was a positive step on the part of the Mexican government, it had no particular effect on the Hopis, since they had virtually no contact with Mexican authorities.

In the early nineteenth century, travelers and traders from the United States began to make their appearance in the Southwest, even though the region was then part of Mexico. American trappers and merchants ventured into New Mexico and Arizona seeking beaver pelts for the profitable domestic and foreign fur markets. Santa Fe became a major regional trading center after 1822, when the Santa Fe Trail was opened. The trail linked the Southwest to the eastern United States and attracted an influx of American traders and settlers throughout the rest of the nineteenth century.

The Hopis, however, remained isolated from trading activity and from interaction with the new intruders. Still, sporadic contact did take place. Although such contact was generally peaceful, conflict also occurred. In one incident, a group of trappers employed by the Rocky Mountain Fur Company looted Hopi farms in 1840. When the Hopis approached the trappers, they were attacked, and between fifteen and twenty Hopis were killed.

After the defeat of Mexico in the Mexican-American War, the territory in which the Pueblo Indians lived became part of the United States under the 1848 Treaty of Guadalupe Hidalgo. U.S. government officials, settlers, and travelers began to arrive in ever-greater numbers. Predictably, as their presence increased, competition over land increased as well. The Hopis and other Pueblos were naturally concerned that the American intruders would encroach on Native lands. In the Treaty of Guadalupe Hidalgo, the United States had pledged to respect the land rights of all former citizens of Mexico, including the Pueblos. But the legal status of the Pueblos in the United States put them in some jeopardy; for whereas the Pueblos had been citizens under the Mexican state, the U.S. government did not grant citizenship to Native peoples but rather considered them wards of the state. As wards, or legal minors, the Pueblos did not have equal standing with Anglo and Hispanic residents. They therefore had to depend on the U.S. government to protect their rights. Unfortunately, this protection was not reliable.

In a move to assert U.S. jurisdiction in the Southwest, the federal *Bureau of Indian Affairs (BIA)* appointed an *agent* to deal with Indians in the area. The bureau had been established in 1824 with the duty of overseeing government policies and programs in Native American communities in the United States. The Southwest agent, John Calhoun, set up regional headquarters for the BIA in Santa Fe in 1850. In October of that year, the Hopis sent a delegation of their leaders to meet with Calhoun. The group was headed by a man named Nakwaiyamtewa, who was a clan leader from the village of Oraibi, then the principal Hopi town. Nakwaiyamtewa and the other Hopi

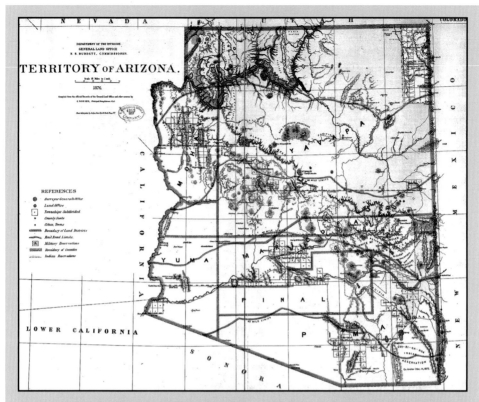

Arizona Territory, c. 1876. Under Mexican rule, the Hopis had held full rights as citizens, but after the 1848 Treaty of Guadalupe Hidalgo ceded Arizona to the United States, the Hopis became wards of the state and did not have equal standing with Anglo and Hispanic residents.

representatives had two goals in mind. First, they wanted to establish friendly relations with the new government administrators. Second, they sought help from the United States in fending off raids by the Navajos and the Utes, which had become more frequent in the early nineteenth century.

Calhoun was sympathetic toward the Hopis' requests and presented them with gifts as tokens of friendship. He told the Hopis that the United States would come to their aid. In 1851, the U.S. government built a fort, called Fort Defiance, in western New Mexico, from which troops were dispatched to fight Navajo and Ute raiders. Although these expeditions helped protect the Hopis, they were of equal benefit to the growing number of Anglo settlers whose farms and ranches were also the targets of Indian raids.

After the establishment of Fort Defiance, U.S. officials visited Hopi villages in 1851 and 1852 to meet with Hopi leaders and to observe conditions in the settlements. These visits were followed by a number of disastrous events. A new wave of smallpox epidemics struck the Hopis in 1853 and 1854, resulting in the deaths of hundreds of people. During the same period, serious droughts occurred, further reducing the population through widespread famine. The population of Oraibi, for instance, declined from approximately eight hundred to only two hundred in just a few years.

Further droughts and outbreaks of smallpox hit the Hopis beginning in 1864. Hopi leaders sought relief from U.S. officials but received little aid. As a result, many Hopis left their towns and took temporary refuge among the Zuñis. As droughts and disease repeatedly struck their villages, the Hopi population fluctuated throughout the nineteenth century. Estimates put the total number of Hopis at between two thousand and three thousand during the century.

During the American Civil War (1861–1865), the U.S. government used its resources to fight the war and therefore devoted little time or material to Indian tribes in the Southwest. Given this situation, raids by the Navajos and the Utes against the Hopis and other Pueblo tribes increased. The raids finally ceased after 1864 when the United States began a brutal policy aimed at controlling the Navajos. The U.S. military was sent to fight the Navajos, killing hundreds, perhaps thousands, of Navajo men, women, and children. Eight thousand Navajos were arbitrarily rounded up by U.S. soldiers and imprisoned at Bosque Redondo, a New Mexico army base. They were held there for four years, from 1864 until 1868. Although the policy restored some measure of security to the Hopis, it also resulted in the deaths of many defenseless Navajos and the destruction of their crops and livestock.

Beginning in the second half of the nineteenth century, several Christian sects undertook missionary activity among the Hopis. Mormons based in Utah began visiting Hopi settlements in 1858. They set up a mission in 1875 at the village of *Moencopi* (MO-en-ko-pi; "flowing-stream place"), a relatively new settlement outside Oraibi. In 1870, another Protestant denomination, the Moravians, established a mission at Oraibi. Baptist and Mennonite missionaries also visited and preached among the Hopis during the same period.

Despite the influx of missionaries, none had any particular success in converting the Hopis. Other changes, however, began to take place; the combined effect of which did transform Hopi life. The BIA opened a Hopi Indian Agency at Oraibi in 1870. Four years later, a second agency was established in a nearby town called Keams Canyon, which had been built by a family of Anglo traders. Keams Canyon began as a trading post and later grew into a regional BIA administrative center. Increasing numbers of Anglo immigrants arrived in the area. Some were government employees; others were ranchers, merchants, missionaries, and teachers.

During the 1870s, construction of railroads linking the east and west coasts of the United States brought still more workers and settlers into the Southwest. One line, the Atchison, Topeka and Santa Fe, ran about seventy-five miles south of Hopi territory. When the railroad was completed in 1881, travelers sometimes stopped off and decided to stay in the region. Towns such as Flagstaff, Winslow, and Holbrook were founded. All were no more than seventy miles from Hopi villages. In addition, in 1878, Mormons (members of the Church of Jesus Christ of Latter-Day Saints) built the town of Tuba City just west of the Hopi mesas. They gradually encroached on Hopi land by expanding their farms and livestock ranges.

The Hopis soon became alarmed at the growing population of Anglos residing in and near their territory. They appealed to U.S. officials for protection against encroachments on their land and harm to their property. In response, President Chester A. Arthur signed an executive order in 1882 that transformed Hopi lands into a protected *reservation*. The reserved land consisted of 2.5 million acres in an area 55-by-70 miles wide. According to the wording of the executive order, the reservation was to be inhabited by "Hopis and other Indians." This wording has recently become extremely significant in disputes between the Hopis and the Navajos over land rights, as we shall see in the next chapter.

Despite increased contact between the Hopis and Anglo newcomers to the region, the Hopi way of life remained essentially unchanged, although some innovations were made. The Hopis adopted some new equipment into their farming technology, including such items as plows, iron hoes, and shovels. They produced their traditional crops of corn, beans, and squash, adding a few foods borrowed from Europeans. These consisted mainly of fruits such as peaches, apples, and melons. The Hopis also began to use wooden doors and glass windows in their houses, although their architecture and village plans followed traditional patterns. In general, the Hopi people prospered in the late nineteenth century. While the Hopis continued to adopt some items from Anglo culture that they considered advantageous, they did not abandon their own way of life nor change their values.

Then in the late 1870s and 1880s, a new government policy began to affect the Hopis. Schools were opened for Hopi children, first at Keams Canyon in 1874 and later in Hopi villages. Some Hopi leaders were willing to have the children attend school, but they also voiced concern over the future of Hopi traditions. In 1886, twenty religious leaders sent a letter to the BIA in Washington, D.C., stating that they wanted their children to "learn the American's tongue and their ways of work. [But] we pray that the children may follow in their parents' footsteps and grow up good of heart and pure of breath."

Other Hopis strongly opposed sending their children to Anglo schools. They were concerned that the children would be taught to follow a way of life vastly different from their traditional culture. They feared that the stability and harmony of their existence were threatened by U.S. educational policies. School officials first tried to entice parents to enroll their children in school by giving them an ax, shovel, or rake as a present. When this tactic failed, authorities arrested Hopi fathers who kept their children at home. The fathers were sentenced to ninety days of hard labor.

In addition, the government sometimes sent soldiers to Hopi villages to round up children and forcibly take them to school. In one particularly disturbing incident that occurred in 1890, soldiers entered a kiva during an initiation rite for boys, disrupted the ceremony, and took all of the boys away.

The Hopis' resentment of the government naturally increased as a result of such actions. Adding to the people's anger, teachers and missionaries criticized Hopi religious practices, which Anglos considered pagan or uncivilized. They convinced government authorities to try to stop the Hopis from performing Native rituals. At this time, the United States did not feel that the guarantee of religious liberty as stated in the Constitution extended to Native Americans. The Hopis responded to this interference in their religious life by conducting their ceremonies in secret. Nonetheless, the government's policies fueled their bitterness about Anglo interference.

Throughout the last years of the nineteenth century and the early years of the twentieth, two opposing factions developed in Hopi communities. One group strongly opposed Anglo intervention in Native life. Its members were alarmed by encroachments on their land by settlers, farmers, and ranchers. They viewed the influx of Anglo traders, missionaries, government workers, and teachers as a threat to their own survival. And they resented that the government imposed policies on them without prior consultation.

The other faction favored cooperation with federal and local authorities. Its members believed that the form of education encouraged by the BIA was advantageous and would lead to prosperity for the Hopis. Many of these people were bilingual and had personal interactions with Anglos through work and casual contact.

Controversies between the two factions worsened by the end of the nineteenth century. People belonging to the opposing groups, dubbed the "Hostiles" and the "Friendlies" in terms of their attitudes toward the U.S. government, disagreed about many issues. The Hostiles opposed all government policies, while the Friendlies often cooperated with official programs. For instance, in the late 1890s, when an outbreak of smallpox hit the village of Shongopavi, Hostiles stopped health workers from entering the town to vaccinate residents and fumigate their houses. The Friendlies at Shongopavi supported the health workers and were angered by the Hostiles' resistance. After heated arguments between the two groups, the Friendlies forced the Hostiles to leave the village.

The Hostiles expelled from Shongopavi were offered refuge by sympathizers in nearby Oraibi. But this move only worsened an already tense situation in Oraibi. People there had long disagreed over whether to send their children to school. This issue became a focus in Oraibi after 1890. In that year, the leader of the Oraibi Friendlies, an influential clan chief named Lololoma, accepted a government invitation to travel to Washington, D.C., to consult with officials there. Lololoma and the chiefs of four other villages who accompanied him were impressed by what they saw and heard in Washington. They returned to their homes, advocating education and other changes in Hopi life. When Lololoma died in 1900, he was succeeded as leader of the Friendlies by a young chief named Tewaquaptewa. The Hostiles, led by a chief named Yokeoma, continued their opposition to schools and other government policies.

When the Hostiles from Shongopavi arrived in Oraibi, people there disagreed about whether to accept the refugees. The factions in Oraibi, led by Tewaquaptewa and Yokeoma, each mustered support from their own lineages and clans. After a while, antagonism between the two factions was so strong that the people could no longer interact with each other. The groups even began to hold their ceremonies in separate kivas. This development was particularly striking in the context of Hopi life. The Hopis had always believed that community rituals were essential to maintaining the strength and solidarity of their villages. Harmony and balance in the universe were therefore threatened when the Hostiles and the Friendlies conducted separate ceremonies.

Village leaders finally realized that all attempts to reach a consensus or compromise were futile. They decided that one faction would have to leave Oraibi in order for peace to be restored. But neither group wanted to leave. So the leaders devised a plan that would force one of the factions out. They said that followers of the two groups should engage in a tug-of-war to decide who would stay in Oraibi and who would leave.

The competition was held on September 8, 1906. Hostiles and Friendlies massed on either side of a line drawn on the ground: Each side grabbed onto a rope strung across the line, then all of the Hopis in Oraibi pulled with all the might they could muster. The Hostiles lost. As a result, their group, numbering 298 people, left Oraibi and set up a new village seven miles away. The village, called *Hotevilla* (HO-te-vee-la; "juniper slope"), is nestled at the foot of Third Mesa. The Friendlies, 324 in number, remained in their natal town.

At the end of the bitter conflict, a young Hopi man named Robert Selena wrote an inscription on a large boulder marking the line drawn on the earth of Oraibi for the tug-of-war. The inscription read:

> Well it have to be done
> This way now
> That when you pass me over the line
> It will be done
> > September 8, 1906

The events at Oraibi show how the Hopis deal with crises. When disagreements first arose, people talked about the issues and tried to convince others to see their point of view. After a while, though, the dispute deepened, and members of each group began to avoid contact with those in the other faction. Such avoidance even led to the separation of religious ceremonies. Finally, when village leaders realized that the people would never be able to agree, they knew that the community could no longer function as a harmonious unit. Without harmony, life was impossible. Leaders also feared that prolonging the dispute might lead to physical violence between opposing groups. The tug-of-war was thus a way of resolving the problem without bloodshed.

By separating their communities, both factions hoped to reestablish harmony in their own villages and live in peace. The twentieth century, however, proved to be a time of change for all peoples.

6

Adjusting to Change

While it is possible to see the conflict at Oraibi in September 1906 as a failure of the Hopis to reconcile their differences, it is important to remember that the root cause of the disagreement was the U.S. government's desire, however well intentioned, to control the Hopis. Although the Hopis had resolved the immediate crisis—albeit at a high price—the problem of not having control over their lives would continue to plague them for the remainder of the century.

Immediately after the Hostiles left Oraibi in September 1906 and moved to Hotevilla, U.S. authorities began to exert control over the new Hopi community. Leaders of the Hostiles, including Yokeoma and other clan chiefs, were arrested and imprisoned at Fort Wingate.

One of the main irritants between the Hopis and the U.S. government continued to be the issue of education. The government chose to focus its energies on education because it believed that if

Hopi children were taught in schools, they would eventually abandon their own cultural traditions and follow instead the Anglo-American way of life.

To accomplish this goal, schools for Hopi children were set up in Keams Canyon rather than in Native villages. This forced the children to live where the schools were and separated them from their families. Every effort was made to strip them of their own culture and to impose Anglo-American culture in its place. Their Hopi clothing was taken away, and they were forced to wear Anglo-style clothing. They were forced to attend Christian religious classes and participate in church services. Finally, they were even forbidden to speak the Hopi language. Children caught speaking Hopi, whether in classrooms, playgrounds, or dormitories, were slapped or whipped.

So intent was the government on carrying out its policy of supplanting Hopi culture that force was used. Soldiers arrived in Hotevilla, rounded up all of the children, and took them to the Keams Canyon school under military escort. In the autobiography of Helen Sekaquaptewa, a Hopi woman who was eight years old at the time, the author relates how the children reacted to their predicament: "Evenings we would gather in a corner and cry softly so that the matron would not hear and scold or spank us. I can still hear the plaintive little voices saying 'I want to go home. I want my mother.'"

Although schoolchildren from most Hopi villages were allowed to return home for summer vacations, boys and girls from Hotevilla were kept in school year-round. The forced separation of Hotevilla parents and children was both a punishment for the parents' objections to government policies and an attempt to wean the children from their own traditions.

Instead of spending their summers at home, speaking their Native language, and participating in Hopi religious life, children from Hotevilla worked in the homes of Keams Canyon's Anglo residents. Government officials, ministers, and traders contracted with the schools for the children's services. Girls carried out domestic tasks such as cleaning and cooking, while boys ran errands and did manual work around the house.

Hopi men who continued to object to the government's actions were arrested and jailed in Keams Canyon. In all, seventy men were sentenced for up to one year of hard labor. Helen Sekaquaptewa noted that she frequently saw her father and the other prisoners walk past the schoolyard on their way to the labor camp. She commented: "They were fastened together in twos with ball and chain. They were not ashamed of their condition because they knew in their hearts they had done nothing wrong; they had only protested having their lives interfered with."

Over the next few years, the government expanded its educational program by opening day schools in Shongopavi and other villages. As before, many parents did not want to send their children to school; and, again, soldiers arrived to escort the children. Once again, the Hopi men who objected were arrested and imprisoned.

Since the schools in Keams Canyon and the Hopi villages only provided education through the sixth grade, older children were sent out of the region to other schools. Most teenagers attended either the Phoenix Indian School in Phoenix, Arizona; the Haskell Institute in Lawrence, Kansas; or the Sherman Indian School in Riverside, California. In addition to offering academic and vocational classes, these schools organized work programs for students in the summertime. Teenagers were hired by agricultural businesses to work as laborers on farms in Colorado and California. (For additional information on these schools, enter "American Indian Boarding Schools" into any search engine and browse the many sites listed.)

Then, in 1939, the first Hopi high school was opened in the village of Oraibi. After that time, teenagers could complete their education locally rather than having to attend distant boarding schools.

Beginning in the late 1800s, the U.S. government adopted a policy of assimilation where it attempted to strip the Hopis of their culture by sending children to schools such as the Phoenix Indian School (shown here). Once they arrived, they were forced to wear Anglo-style clothing, attend Christian religious classes and participate in church services, and were even forbidden to speak the Hopi language.

During the early years of the twentieth century, the federal government introduced a variety of other programs on the Hopi Reservation. In 1913, a hospital was opened in Keams Canyon for treatment of Hopi and Navajo Indians. Clinics staffed by nurses and doctors on a rotating basis were started in some of the villages. Other government projects addressed economic conditions on the Hopi Reservation. In an attempt to improve agricultural production, the government provided funds for drilling wells and for building irrigation ditches and flood-control dikes. Finally, in response to an outbreak of skin disease among the sheep owned by Hopi herders, a program of sheep-dipping was started in the late 1920s. Once a year, owners of livestock took their sheep to sheep-dips where the

The snake legend, depicted here, is the basis for the Hopi snake ceremony. The story tells of a chief's son's epic journey to find out where the Colorado River winds up. During his trip, he ventures to the underworld, travels across the sky, and comes to realize the importance of the rain-cloud.

Hopi artists painted dramatic murals on walls of buildings that they used for conducting ceremonies. Multicolor paintings depicted scenes of animals, humans, and mythological figures, such as this Fertility God.

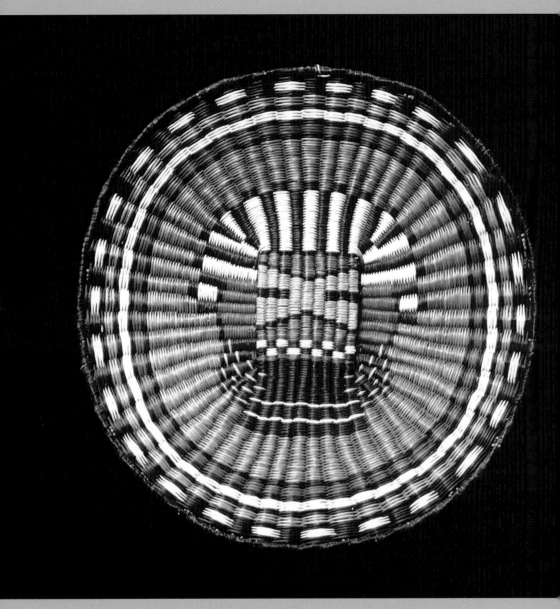

Hopi wicker plaques are traditionally made by women of Third Mesa villages, which include Oraibi, Kykotsmovi, Hotevilla, and Bacavi, and are often very colorful thanks to the use of native plants and dyes.

A Hopi hand-coiled pot. Hopi pottery is greatly valued, but almost became a lost art until a First Mesa woman named Nampeyo revived the practice in the late 1800s.

Wood-carved dolls like this one represent the spirits of ancestors (kachinas) who are revered for their ability to bring rain for the spring crops.

A wood figurine representing a kachina spirit. According to Hopi tradition, kachinas visit Hopi villages at sunrise and bring presents of food and other items to the residents, who respond with thanks and prayers.

Shalako Mana, represented here as a wood carving, is the female companion of the Shalako kachina and is representative of all the breath of the Hopi ancestors who create clouds and bring rain to Hopi lands.

Hopi deer dancers take part in kachina ceremonies as another way to bring clouds and rain for the spring crops.

animals were washed with a medicinal solution to protect them from infection.

Federal policy toward Native Americans took an important new direction in the 1930s. A few years before, in 1928, a national survey of reservations (the Meriam Report) had documented high levels of poverty, malnutrition, and disease in Native American communities. In response, funds for reservations were increased and efforts were made to address local problems.

After Franklin Delano Roosevelt became president in 1933, he placed John Collier at the head of the BIA. Collier was a man with a deep knowledge of and appreciation for Native Americans, and he genuinely wanted to use the BIA to help them. Under the direction of its new commissioner, the BIA pressed Congress for passage of the *Indian Reorganization Act* (IRA). When the IRA was passed in 1934, it provided for a limited degree of self-government on federal Indian reservations. Each community was empowered to adopt a constitution, elect a tribal council, and participate in developing local programs. Although in actual practice local independence was severely restricted, the IRA at least recognized Native American rights to land. It also encouraged the continuation of traditional ways of life.

After passage of the IRA, according to the act's provisions, a referendum was held in Hopi villages so that people could express either their support for or opposition to accepting the act's provisions. The overwhelming majority of the Hopis refused to participate in the referendum. By staying away from the vote, most Hopis showed their disapproval of the entire process. But of those who did vote, most favored the IRA. The act then went into effect: A tribal council was elected in 1935, and a formal constitution was adopted the following year.

Even though the IRA was officially accepted, controversies arose within the Hopi community over the issue of community leadership. In a continuation of the two divergent attitudes the

Hopis had earlier taken toward cooperation with the U.S. government, this split in opinion found new expression in response to the IRA. One group of Hopis, called the *Progressives*, supported the system of elected representatives. Another faction, called the *Traditionals*, wanted to maintain clan chiefs as the legitimate local leaders. Two systems of leadership therefore coexist in Hopi villages.

During the 1930s, the BIA began a program to reduce the amount of livestock owned by Hopi and Navajo herders. The stock-reduction policy was a response to the problem of soil erosion on the reservations. Although Collier genuinely wanted to improve conditions for the Hopis and the Navajos, the program was poorly designed and unfairly implemented. Members of the affected communities were not consulted before the policy was put into effect. The Hopis and the Navajos were shocked and angered when they were told that they would have to surrender up to half of their sheep. When they objected to the program, government officials told them that they had no power to change the policies.

A serious flaw in the program was that although the government paid owners for their sheep, the market price for sheep brought to slaughter was not equal to their real value. Most Hopis did not ordinarily sell their sheep for food but rather kept them for the wool they produced. If a sheep is sheared every year, its owner keeps receiving an income from the sale of wool. In contrast, if a sheep is sold, money is only earned once. By paying herders the market rate, the government did not actually compensate the Hopis and the Navajos for the full potential value of their sheep.

The entire experience of stock reduction left a permanent mark on relations between the Hopis and the federal government. It again raised the issue of local control over community life and well-being. The Hopis felt that their opinions and interests had been ignored, and they saw the program as another example of government interference.

John Collier (right), who was appointed Commissioner of Indian Affairs in 1933 by President Franklin Delano Roosevelt, was an advocate for fair treatment of Native Americans. Although many of Collier's proposals did not win the backing of Congress, the Indian Reorganization Act of 1934 was a step in the right direction in that it called for tribal self-government and the return of individual land allotments to tribes.

In 1948, the bureau began another policy that proved to be unpopular. The BIA opened the *Branch of Relocation*; the goal of which was to relocate Native Americans from reservations to cities throughout the United States. Few jobs were available on or near most reservations, and the relocation program was an attempt to alleviate the resultant unemployment. One of the stated intentions of the relocation program was to help Indians obtain jobs in urban centers. The Branch of Relocation supplied funds for transportation from reservations to cities and in some cases paid for job training. But once again, the BIA had not asked the Hopis or other Native Americans what they wanted.

Indians from all reservations were included in the program. The Hopis were encouraged to enroll and relocate to such western cities as Phoenix, Arizona; Denver, Colorado; and Los Angeles, California. But very few Hopis agreed to relocate. Most preferred to continue farming and raising their sheep or to try to seek jobs in nearby non-Hopi towns.

In fact, the relocation program proved to be a dismal failure throughout the United States. Although it was officially aimed at improving economic conditions for Native Americans, most Indians who moved to cities found themselves jobless and living in decaying urban ghettos. The large majority of people who did agree to relocate eventually returned to their reservations, finding that they preferred to live on their own land where they could find emotional and material support in their own communities.

In 1950, Congress passed the Navajo-Hopi Act, which allotted a sum of $88 million for improvements on both reservations. The funds paid for the construction of wells, fences, roads, and flood-control dikes. Although the money was put to good use, many traditional leaders continued to object to government interference in their lives.

By the middle of the twentieth century, concern grew among many Hopis over the issue of loss of their original territory. In 1949, twenty-four Traditionals sent a letter to authorities in Washington, D.C., expressing their convictions about the importance of land. They said: "This land is the sacred home of the Hopi people. It was given to the Hopi people the task to guard this land by obedience to our traditional and religious instructions. We have never abandoned our sovereignty to any foreign power or nation."

Hopi leaders appealed to the federal *Indian Claims Court*, founded in 1946, to investigate Hopi claims to land they considered theirs. The suit, filed in 1950, stated that land had been illegally sold from the territory promised to the Hopis in the 1882 executive order that had established their reservation.

In addition to the problem of land lost through sales and encroachment by settlers, another factor that contributed to the reduction of the Hopis' land base grew out of the wording of the 1882 executive order that established the Hopi Reservation. That order set aside land for the "Hopis and other Indians." Among the "other Indians" were the Navajos, whose territory was adjacent to that of the Hopis. Many Navajos gradually moved onto land located within the borders of the original Hopi Reservation. Since the Navajo population had grown quickly, they sought additional acreage for sheep grazing and farming. The BIA allowed the Navajos to move onto the Hopi lands since this did not violate the original executive order. But the Navajos' presence naturally worried the Hopis, who feared that their rights to land would one day be endangered.

In the 1950s, the Hopis and the Navajos began negotiations over the issue of land rights. Federal authorities became involved and recommended a court review of the problem. In 1962, a panel of three judges granted the Hopis exclusive use of the area consisting of their villages and the immediate surrounding land. This area, called *District Six*, contained 631,306 acres of the original 2.5-million-acre reservation. In the remaining portion of the Hopi Reservation, the Hopis and the Navajos were given "joint, undivided and equal rights."

The wording of the court's decision was unfortunately just as vague and unsatisfactory as that of the 1882 executive order. By stating that the two groups had "joint and undivided" rights to land, the problem of where people would settle and farm and where they could graze their sheep was not resolved. Joint administration of land by the Hopis and the Navajos proved to be cumbersome and led to conflict. Indeed, conflict over land rights continued to plague the Hopis and the Navajos for many years. In one attempt to solve the problem, the Navajo Tribal Council in 1970 offered to pay the Hopis for outright purchase of the so-called joint-use area in which both Hopis and Navajos lived.

This proposal angered the Hopis because it implied that they would be willing to sell their rights to their ancestral territory.

After more controversy and negotiations between the Hopi and Navajo tribes, the federal government again stepped in to resolve the problem. In 1974, Congress passed the *Navajo-Hopi Settlement Act,* which provided for the division of the joint-use area. The act, amended in 1978 and 1988, divided the joint-use area evenly between the two tribes. Each tribe received approximately 911,000 acres for its exclusive use. People who found themselves living on land assigned to the other tribe were given a period of five years to move. The federal government supplied funds for relocation and for purchasing additional land for the Navajos. In general, the Hopis have responded more favorably to the decision than have the Navajos. Because relatively few Hopis were living on land given to the Navajos, few Hopis' lives were disrupted.

In addition to problems over land claims and land use, the Hopis have disagreed over the direction of economic development in their communities. Beginning in 1961, the Hopi Tribal Council agreed to lease land to U.S. companies for production of oil, gas, and minerals. One of the largest projects was started in 1966 by the Peabody Coal Company. Peabody sought and obtained a lease to carry out strip-mining for coal in Black Mesa. The lease provides that the Hopi tribe receive royalties of $500,000 per year. But many Traditionals strongly opposed the project because they saw it as a violation of their sacred trust to protect their land. Traditionals noted that strip-mining has a very destructive effect on land. Although the Peabody Company promised to revitalize the land after mining operations ceased, Traditionals did not believe that such pledges were realistic. They also objected to Peabody's plans to use water beneath Black Mesa in their mining procedures. Traditionals knew that water is a precious resource in Hopi territory and feared that Peabody's use would interfere with farming.

As an outgrowth of their concerns, Traditional chiefs from ten of the thirteen Hopi villages filed suit in 1971 to block Peabody's mining operations. The suit also named the U.S. Department of the Interior and the BIA as codefendants along with Peabody. The plaintiffs argued that the BIA reneged on its obligations to protect Indian lands and rights. The chiefs' statement in the suit echoed the words of their Hopi forebears regarding the importance of land and tradition: "If the land is abused, the sacredness of Hopi life will disappear."

The Traditionals also claimed that the Hopi Tribal Council had no authority to dispose of Hopi land. Since only a small number of Hopis voted in tribal elections, Traditionals did not acknowledge the council as representative of the Hopi people or of their interests.

Although the legal suit against Peabody was denied, Traditionals believed that it was important to raise the issues of leadership and sovereignty. The Hopis may have different opinions about these topics, but they agree that all people should have the right to decide how to govern themselves and how to conduct their lives. These are ancient values, kept alive by countless generations.

7

The Modern Hopis

The lives of the Hopi people today are, of course, vastly different from those of their ancestors who lived centuries ago. External conditions have changed, but with the possible exception of the Zuñis, the Hopis have been able to maintain more of their cultural traditions and values than any other tribe of Native Americans.

The principles of harmony and balance, so important to the strength and survival of Hopi communities, remain as guiding ideals for the people today. Don Talayesva, a Hopi chief of the Sun Clan, recalls in his autobiography the wise words of his uncle who taught him to respect the ancient ways:

Put your trust in the Cloud People. They come from the six directions to examine our hearts. If we are good, they gather above us in cotton masks and white robes and drop rain to quench our thirst and nourish our plants. Rain is what we need most and when the gods see fit they can pour it on us. Keep bad thoughts behind you and face the rising sun with a cheerful spirit, as did our ancestors in the days of plenty. Work hard, keep the ceremonies, live peaceably, and unite your heart with ours so that our messages will reach the Cloud People. Then maybe they will pity us and drop the rains on our fields.

These words express the timeless values of the Hopis. Still, even for the Hopis, the practical reality of life has changed. Most Hopis no longer support themselves exclusively by the traditional pursuit of farming. Instead, many Hopis gain their livelihood from wage work or from combinations of wages, farming, and raising livestock. Members of a family often pursue different kinds of work, all contributing their share of wages, income, or produce to the household.

Still, farming remains an important element in the Hopi economy. The traditional staples of corn, beans, and squash are still planted and highly prized. In addition, Hopi farmers grow melons, other varieties of fruit, and wheat. Many families keep a stock of sheep, goats, and cattle. They sell wool from the sheep at local markets. Dairy and beef cattle also provide some income.

Hopi families utilize the produce from their farms and livestock in their own households. They may also sell surplus crops and goods at local markets. Trading and selling to nearby Navajos is another source of income for the Hopis.

Since the middle of the twentieth century, wage work has become a greater part of the Hopi economy. Various kinds of employment are available in surrounding towns near the reservation. Men often work as construction workers, carpenters, and in other building trades. Women tend to obtain jobs as waitresses, clerks, secretaries, and maids. Still other Hopis find employment in a variety of capacities with the Hopi Tribal Council and federal agencies such as the BIA. Schools, health-care facilities, and

Today, raising livestock plays an important part in both generating income for the Hopis and providing sustenance for individual families. Many Hopi families keep a stock of sheep, goats, and cattle and often sell wool from the sheep at local markets.

tribal enterprises provide jobs for a small but growing number of people.

Although many villages maintain their basic traditional plan, some new towns have been founded. These towns reflect changes in Hopi life. For example, the town of Moencopi began as an outgrowth of the old village of Oraibi in the late nineteenth century. It has a rather unusual legal status. Although it is a Hopi town, it is located outside of the area designated as the Hopi Reservation by the 1882 executive order. Despite its location, Moencopi was administered by the BIA's Hopi Agency in Keams Canyon. In 1900, when the boundaries of the Navajo Reservation were set, Moencopi found itself within Navajo territory. Nonetheless, it remained under the jurisdiction of the Hopi Agency.

Moencopi residents rely on a mixed economy of farming, sheepherding, and wage work. Although few jobs are available in the town itself, residents seek work in nearby Tuba City, located two miles away. Tuba City was founded by Mormons in the 1870s and has grown to a population of more than eight thousand (as of 2000). Most of its permanent residents are Navajos, although Hopis and Anglos also live there.

The Hopis in Moencopi shop in stores and seek services available in Tuba City. They also travel seventy miles away from the reservation to the larger center of Flagstaff for shopping and for employment. Some Hopis attend schools in either Tuba City or Flagstaff. They may also seek medical treatment or other services there.

Although towns like Tuba City and Flagstaff provide some jobs and services for the Hopis, serious economic problems persist for the Hopi Nation. Most businesses are owned by outsiders, especially Anglos. Anglos are also the main providers of services as well as the administrators employed by government agencies. The Hopis tend to be concentrated in low-paying, unskilled, and temporary jobs.

One village on the Hopi Reservation that has an unusual history is that of Hano, one of three towns situated on First Mesa. Hano was founded in 1696 by Tewa people who previously had lived in pueblos along the Rio Grande in New Mexico. They had fought against the Spanish in the Pueblo Revolt of 1680. When the Spanish reconquered New Mexico twelve years later, a group of Tewa decided to leave their homes and resettle among the Hopis in Arizona.

The Tewas and the Hopis have somewhat different accounts of the events that led to the Tewas' arrival at the Hopi mesas in 1696. According to the Hopis, the Tewas asked to join Hopi communities and offered to help protect them against attacks from Spaniards or raids by the Navajos and Utes. The

Tewas' version of how they came to live among the Hopis is quite different. The Tewas say that the Hopis sent a delegation to the Tewa village in New Mexico to ask the Tewas to come to their aid. The Hopis knew of the Tewas' reputation as skilled warriors and wanted their help in fending off Navajo raids. The Hopi leaders promised to give them a good place to build their houses and much land on which to plant their crops. The Tewa chiefs accepted the offer and led their families westward. When they arrived in Hopi territory, the Hopis refused to allow them into their villages and the Hopis did not treat the Tewas with the respect they had promised but instead insulted and ridiculed them. Finally, after the Tewas defeated a group of Ute raiders who came to raid Hopi fields, Hopi leaders agreed to let the Tewas remain. They gave their protectors a portion of land on First Mesa. The Tewa village of Hano is located at the tip of the Mesa where the road descends to the desert below. It shares First Mesa with two Hopi villages, Sichomovi and Walpi.

The Tewas' story of their arrival in Hopi territory continues with an account of a curse that Tewa leaders put on the Hopis because of the rude treatment they received:

> Our clan chiefs dug a pit between Hano and the Hopi villages on First Mesa and told the Hopi clan chiefs to spit into it. When they had all spat, our clan chiefs spat above the spittle of the Hopis. The pit was refilled, and then our clan chiefs declared: "Because you have behaved in a manner unbecoming to human beings, we have sealed knowledge of our language and our way of life from you. You and your descendants will never learn our language and our ceremonies, but we will learn yours. We will ridicule you both in your language and our own."

Whatever the initial motivation, the Tewas came to live in Hopi territory and built their village at the top of First Mesa in 1696. From this vantage point, they successfully defended First Mesa against enemy intruders. When Spanish soldiers tried to attack the Hopis in the early eighteenth century, the Tewas helped defeat them.

In one incident that occurred in 1716, a Spanish expedition arrived in Hopi territory to try to convince the Tewas at Hano to return to their Rio Grande pueblos. When the Tewas refused, Spanish soldiers fired on them, killing eight people. As they departed, the Spaniards destroyed the crops in the Tewas' fields.

In addition to defending the community from Spanish armies, the Tewas used their military skills to defend First Mesa against Navajo and Ute raiders.

The Tewas and the Hopis have lived near each other on First Mesa since 1696. Despite this geographical proximity, their villages have remained distinct. As an indication of their social separation, the Hopis and the Tewas conduct rituals in their own kivas. Although the Tewas have maintained a strong sense of their unique cultural identity, they have also borrowed some Hopi customs. For instance, while the Tewas in New Mexico do not have a strong clan system, those at Hano have adopted matrilineal clans like those of the Hopis. In addition, like the Hopis, Tewa households are matrilineal.

For two centuries after the Tewas arrived at First Mesa, they and the Hopis did not intermarry. By the beginning of the twentieth century, women and men from the two groups occasionally married. Today, approximately half of all Tewa men and women have Hopi spouses. Following the current custom of both peoples, married men move to their wives' households. Although relations between families of an intermarried couple are friendly and cooperative, Hopi men living in Tewa households typically do not speak the Tewa language. Since all Tewas are bilingual, Tewa men residing among the Hopis speak Hopi, but the Hopis never learn Tewa. The people today are thus living out the curse put on the Hopis by Tewa clan leaders centuries ago.

The course of history of the Tewas at Hano followed a path similar to that of the Hopis. In the nineteenth and twentieth centuries, they faced the same challenges from intruders and from U.S. officials pressuring them to give up their traditional way of life. Since the Tewas had a long history of intermingling with different groups, many of them were quick to learn English. They often served as interpreters between the Hopis and Anglos. As their history had made them adaptable, the Tewas were often more willing than their Hopi neighbors to adopt educational and economic changes introduced by U.S. authorities.

The population of Hano has continued to grow, as has the population of Hopi villages. The three First Mesa towns of Hano, Sichomovi, and Walpi each have approximately 550 residents. A second Tewa village was established at the foot of First Mesa in 1888. It is named Polacca, after its founder, Tom Polacca, who was an influential Tewa leader.

Economic development on the Hopi Reservation is growing, but it is still limited. In the 1970s, the tribe opened a complex consisting of a motel, restaurant, craft shop, and museum. The center, located on Second Mesa, attracts visitors and people interested in purchasing Hopi crafts.

Hopi arts have become quite popular throughout the United States. One specialty is traditional Hopi pottery. Although Hopi women made pottery long ago, the craft died out in the seventeenth century. Then, in the late 1800s, a woman named Nampeyo from the village of Hano studied ancient earthen bowls, dishes, and jars found in prehistoric Hopi sites. She began to produce pottery using traditional materials and designs. Since then, other Hopi artisans have taken up the craft of pottery. Their work is highly prized. (For additional information on this master potter, enter "Nampeyo" into any search engine and browse the many sites listed.)

A number of other Hopi artists, sculptors, and silversmiths have gained recognition for their skills. Among these are the painter Fred Kabotie and silversmiths Otellie and Charles Loloma. Charles Loloma is famous for his innovative and striking designs in silver, turquoise, and shell jewelry.

During the late nineteenth century, a Hopi woman named Nampeyo (shown here) revived the lost art of Hopi pottery. She began reproducing ancient pottery in the Sikyatki style, which is characterized by geometric figures and pictures of animals and faces, and she is credited with the creation of the Hano polychrome style.

Although some Hopis have moved from the reservation to either nearby or distant cities, the population of Hopi villages has increased throughout this century. In 1900, the population was between 2,000 and 2,500. By 1950, the number had risen to approximately 4,400, and by 1980, it had increased to 6,591. Population statistics for 2000 indicate a total of 6,946 Hopi living on the reservation. There are slightly more women than men: 3,548 women and 3,398 men. The community is relatively young, having a median age of 29.1 years. There are also a substantial number of elders, totaling 651 individuals who are 65 years of age or older.

Federal statistics on household composition indicate that there are 1,866 housing units occupied on the reservation. Most households (1,468) consist of either a traditional extended group of relatives, a married couple, a couple and their children, or a single parent and children. A small number of houses (231) are occupied by a single person. The proportion of total households consisting of families is higher among the Hopis than among the general U.S. population. This demographic evidence that the Hopis have maintained strong communal and kinship bonds is further proof of the continuity of traditional Hopi values.

An eloquent summation of the Hopi religion and of how the Hopis see their dilemma as an ancient culture struggling to exist under the dominion of another, more powerful culture is given in a statement made in 1954 by Andrew Hermequaftewa, the Bluebird Chief of the village of Shongopavi:

> Our religious teachings are based upon the proper care of our land and the people who live upon it. We must not lose this way of life if we are to remain Hopis, The Peaceful.
>
> We were told that if we accept any other way of life we will so bring trouble upon ourselves. Our forefathers told us this, and their forefathers before them. We believe that if you [the United States government] continue with the present policy, our land will be gone and our way of life will be destroyed. You have marvelous intentions; but many of these seem to lead only to destruction of the Hopi Way.
>
> Many things were prophesied to us, and are being fulfilled today. If we forsake our Hopi religion the land will forsake us. There will be no more Hopi Way, no more Hopi people, nor more peace.
>
> We, the Hopi leaders, want to sit with you and consider all these ancient teachings, the advice that has come to us from our ancestors, and the effects upon our way of life of the

white man's power that is in Washington. We do not want to see the Hopi Way destroyed.

I ask, as a Hopi, as the Bluebird-Chief, will you in Washington who are in authority come and hold council with us? We would stop this loss of our land and destruction of what we have chosen as our way of life. We want to live as Hopis and worship the way we have been doing since the beginning. The Hopi religion is a way of peace that must be shared with all people. May we so share this with you? That is all.

8

Hopis in the Twenty-First Century

As the Hopis enter the twenty-first century, they are confronted by many of the same problems faced by most other Native Americans. They want to secure their rights to their land and improve the economic conditions of their people. But even in the midst of difficulties, the Hopis strongly maintain their faith in their heritage and spiritual beliefs, and they focus on transmitting their language and culture to future generations.

The Hopis are deeply concerned about protecting their land and resources. They continue to negotiate with the neighboring Navajo Nation and with the federal government over territory disputed between the two Native nations. As the latest measure in a prolonged intervention, Congress passed the Navajo-Hopi Land Dispute Settlement Act in 1996. This law updated the original legislation enacted in 1974. Its purpose was to clarify the procedures for relocating Navajos and Hopis who were living on land assigned to the other group. However, critical issues have yet to be resolved. There is debate among the people about whether the disputed territory has been divided fairly and in the best interest of both tribes. The people are also concerned about the acquisition of new land for tribal members who have been displaced from their former homes. Although a greater number of Navajos were told to relocate, many Hopi families also had to move from territory that they and their families have lived on for generations. The Hopi Tribal Government has pursued its desire to obtain additional land to help displaced Hopi people. (For additional information on the disputed territory between the Navajos and Hopis, enter "Navajo-Hopi Land Dispute" into any search engine and browse the many sites listed.)

These issues, as well as others concerning the people's well-being, were raised at a meeting between the Hopi Tribal president, Wayne Taylor, Jr., and Arizona Governor Janet Napolitano in 2002. President Taylor stated the Hopis' request for acquiring public land held in trust by the state of Arizona. This land would be used for Hopi families who were forced to move from their previous homes. The Hopi also want to acquire public land in nearby Homolovi State Park. Although the federal government originally gave the Navajos and Hopis until February 1, 2000, to sign agreements to move from the disputed area, several dozen Navajo families continue to resist relocation. Leaders of the Hopi and Navajo Nations have agreed to allow the Navajo families to lease land from the Hopis for seventy-five years. The Navajo families who remain on Hopi land, however, must adhere to Hopi laws. Although no action has been taken on the Hopis' request for additional state land, Governor Napolitano stressed her desire to address the concerns of the Hopis and other indigenous peoples in Arizona. She promised to work with them on issues of land and access to water as well.

Indeed, protection of water resources in the arid Southwest is of critical importance to the Hopi economy and to the survival

Arizona Governor Janet Napolitano has pledged to work closely with the Native tribes who call Arizona home. In addition to working hand-in-hand with them on environmental issues and access to water, she also championed the cause to rename Phoenix's Squaw Peak, Piestewa Peak, in honor of U.S. Army Pfc. Lori Piestewa, a Hopi from Tuba City who was killed while on duty in Iraq in 2003.

of their people. A severe drought in the western and south-western United States that began in the late 1990s is a cause of great concern. The Hopis and other tribal peoples fear that most of the available water resources will be monopolized by the large cities in the West and Southwest whose residents have more political clout than Native peoples. Governor Napolitano pledged to consult with the Hopi and other Indian tribes before appointing state officials to positions of authority over water resources and land.

The Hopis have formed an alliance with the Navajos, aimed at protecting territory that both peoples consider sacred. They are especially focused on a group of mountains called the San Francisco Peaks that are said to be part of the sacred boundaries of the original Hopi and Navajo territories. These mountains contain holy sites where Hopi and Navajo spirit beings long ago emerged from inside the earth. Although the mountains are controlled by the U.S. Forest Service, a ski resort area called Snowball is currently operating on the peaks. The owners of the resort have plans to expand their facilities in order to attract more visitors. The Hopis and Navajos have appealed to the Forest Service, asking that the expansion of Snowball be halted. The Hopis want the region, which they call Nuvatukyaovi (the Hopi name for San Francisco Peaks), to be put on the National Register of Historic Places. Sites on this list receive federal protection against destruction or over-development. Since 1979, the Hopis have strenuously opposed any development at Nuvatukyaovi. They are now asking both for a ban on future development and for the removal of the existing ski facilities.

The Hopis and Navajos also object to plans by the operators of Snowball to utilize wastewater in the making of artificial snow so that the skiing period can be extended into the spring season when natural snow is no longer abundant. The tribes do not want the skiing season to be extended. But they also object to the use of wastewater due to their fears that existing groundwater resources, already scarce in the region, will be contaminated and polluted. They depend upon this water both for drinking and for irrigating their fields during the growing season. Hopi and Navajo leaders oppose the use of wastewater because of its impurities. They see it as a sign of disrespect for the sacred mountain and for the spirits living there. In the words of Hopi Raleigh Puhuyaoma, the use of wastewater on the mountain is like "pumping dirty water on somebody's face. The Katsinas [Hopi spirit beings] and other people are living over there." Raymond Maxx, a member of the Navajo Nation Council, referred to important Navajo shrines on the San Francisco Peaks: "Just the other day my father was out there gathering herbs. Wastewater is sewer water. That's what it is to us. If you allow this to happen, our people will have heavy hearts."

Other Hopi leaders point to the importance of the San Francisco Peaks to Hopi spirituality and to the people's sense of who they are. In the words of Elliott Selestewa, Jr.: "You remember who you are. I can never be a White man. I am who I am. I was a Hopi when I was born. When I die I will be a Hopi; I will go home to the mountain as a spirit to bring rain for my people." Lisa Talayumptewa remarked, "Our elders tell us that everything has life. We all need private time. The beings on the mountain need private time, not noise all day and all night. [The Forest Service says they] can accommodate our views. We don't need accommodation."

Finally, in the Hopis' understanding of the world, one action affects other actions. They perceive a cause-and-effect process in the relationship between people and natural forces. As a result, they interpret the ongoing drought in the Southwest as a result of human actions, not just a simple climatic change. As Elliott Selestewa noted, "Today there is no rain, no snow. We are taught there is a reason for that. The White man doesn't understand the way things work. Maybe the Creator is saying it's high time I speak to everyone on the planet."

In their efforts to protect their resources, the Hopis sponsor annual Water Fairs, bringing together people from different cultures to discuss issues that surround the availability and protection of sources of clean water. At the Water Fair in 2003, researchers and activists from Mexico, Japan, and several Native nations of North America shared their experiences and knowledge. Members of the Tohono O'odham Nation, an indigenous group from southwestern Arizona, discussed their attempts to stop a mining company from using underground water that supplies the reservation community. Other people in the United States and Mexico are waging similar battles against large companies that want to profit from Native resources. In the words of Vernon Masayesva, executive director of the Hopis' Black Mesa Trust: "The next fifty years will determine whether we make the earth strong and healthy again or whether we completely destroy it. That is why some of us are no longer hesitant to share our ancient knowledge with the world."

In addition to environmental and resource issues, governmental reorganization is of major concern to the Hopi Nation. The Hopi Tribal Council has begun to revise the local form of government. A committee appointed by the tribe has written a new constitution for consideration by the tribal council and all of the members of the Hopi tribe. A tribal referendum will be scheduled so that residents can register their approval or disapproval of the proposed constitution. If approved, the major emphasis in the new document is a distribution of more local power to each of the twelve villages that make up the Hopi Nation. There will also be a new system of checks and balances between the executive and legislative bodies. In addition, the constitution will allow each village to decide what form of local government it wants so that it best suits their particular values, traditions, and modern needs. This plan is in keeping with ancient Hopi traditions of village autonomy and independence. Of course, the villages will continue to be united as one tribe with a central coordinating government, but local communities will have a great deal of independence in planning and implementing programs for their village.

Many Hopis continue to engage in farming despite living in an arid region, which has been made worse by the drought that has plagued the Southwest since the late 1990s. Hopi farmers rely on rainfall to water their crops because they are situated far from any natural sources of abundant water. Because of their location, they cannot use irrigation systems to bring them water from other regions. But many Hopis rely on farming to help feed their families. By farming and growing their own crops, Hopis connect to their land and reenact spiritual ties to mother earth. They believe that they have been given their land from the ancient period of creation, and they believe that it is their role and their duty to protect it. The land gives to them through the growth of corn and other plants, while they are sustained by the earth and their work upon it.

Small businesses, especially grocery stores, gas stations, and other retail outlets are also important fixtures in the Hopi landscape. These stores and businesses create jobs for Hopi residents. They also make goods available for people to buy and provide services that help improve people's lives. And through sales, they generate income for the business owners as well.

Many Hopis participate in the production and sale of crafts, especially pottery and jewelry. Hopi artisans sell necklaces, bracelets, rings, and other jewelry to retail outlets on the reservation, in stores in Arizona and the Southwest, and throughout the United States and the world. However, in recent years, Hopi jewelry makers have become increasingly concerned about the production and sale of imitation jewelry made in foreign countries, which is passed off as being made by American Indians. Federal and state laws are aimed at preventing fraudulent marketing claims, but these statutes are rarely enforced in the jewelry market. Fake American Indian jewelry severely undercuts the Hopi market because it is mass produced cheaply in factories in foreign countries where employees are paid very low wages. Authentic Hopi and other Native American crafts which require tremendous skill and time to produce are understandably expensive.

The Hopis and other southwestern Native artisans have appealed to federal and state authorities to crack down on the illegal sale of fake jewelry. They have formed the Council for Indigenous Arts and Culture, based in the nearby Zuñi Reservation, in order to protect their cultural, artistic, and commercial interests. In the words of Andy Abeita, president of the Council for Indigenous Arts and Culture: "Our very way of life is in danger. Our culture, our religion, our language—all these have to do with the arts and crafts we create."

As part of efforts to highlight and publicize authentic Native arts, Hopi artisans participated in a Hopi Arts Festival in San Francisco in 2003. Jewelers and potters displayed their crafts, while musicians and dancers performed for the public. Hopi jewelers now combine traditional and modern patterns and materials to create innovative styles. Some use their work to bring attention to ancient Hopi themes. In the words of jeweler Bennard Dallasvuyaoma, describing his work representing corn pollen, "With this power of harmony in each gem, and the gem's representation of corn pollen, I create my art as a renaissance of my ancient Pima and Hopi ancestry."

Despite some economic problems on the reservation, the Hopi population has steadily increased. According to statistics reported by the Hopi Tribal Council, in 2003, there were 11,323 members of the Hopi tribe. This figure represents a growth rate of 5.5 percent per year. Tribal officials project a population growth of 2.2 percent in the future, lower than the current rate but still strong enough to secure the continuation of the community. They estimate that there will be more than 15,000 tribal members by the year 2020. However, according to the 2000 U.S. Census Bureau's report, there were 6,946 residents living on the Hopi Reservation. If both of these sets of figures are accurate, it means that more than 4,000 tribal members do not live on the reservation. This is probably about the norm for other Native American nations as well. That is, about one-fourth to one-half of tribal members do not live on their tribe's reservations. Most of the people who move away do so because of poor economic conditions and few job opportunities in their home territories.

Nearly all of the residents of the Hopi Reservation are Hopis. They constitute 94.6 percent of the population. Most of the remaining residents are white. Some of these individuals are married to Hopi people, while others operate stores or work in Native villages.

The median age of the Hopi is 29.1 years. As a community, they are therefore somewhat younger than the rest of the United States as a whole. The general U.S. median age is 35 years. The youthfulness of the Hopis is consistent with trends found on other reservations. American Indian communities tend to be somewhat younger than the general U.S. population because they have higher fertility rates. This means that they have more children and larger families. In fact, the U.S. Census Bureau reports an average family size of 4.07 among the Hopis. This figure is significantly higher than the general U.S. average family size of 2.61 individuals.

Education on the Hopi Reservation is a primary concern of tribal officials. The tribe operates six elementary schools, one boarding school, and one school that combines junior and senior high school students. According to the 2000 U.S. Census, 29.9 percent of Hopi tribal members are high school graduates. Another 6.4 percent have graduated from a four-year college. In addition, 4.7 percent have associate degrees, while 3.8 percent have graduate or professional degrees.

In order to support students who wish to continue their education after high school, the Hopi tribe offers its members scholarships to pay for tuition and other college or technical school expenses. Hopi officials and educators are working with other southwestern Native tribes and with colleges in Arizona to increase the numbers of Native applicants to colleges and universities. They are also attempting to discover and address the reasons for the high rate of Native dropouts from institutions of higher education. Caleb Johnson, vice chair of the Hopi tribe, has suggested the development of a think tank dedicated to understanding the economic and cultural factors involved in Native students' attendance at and performance in college.

Residents of the Hopi Reservation continue to face economic difficulties. The Hopi tribal government collects and disseminates information concerning the economic condition of tribal members. The data released by the tribe differ somewhat from that collected by the U.S. Census Bureau, but in both cases, income and employment statistics reveal serious problems, especially when compared with the figures that represent the general U.S. population. The following table displays the relevant data collected by the census in 2000:

	Median Family Income	Per-Capita Income
Hopis	$22,989	$8,531
United States	$46,737	$27,203
Arizona	$34,751	$24,206

These data reveal that Hopi incomes are substantially below U.S. averages and the average for Arizona, the state in which the Hopi Reservation is located. The U.S. median family income is more than twice the Hopi figure, while the U.S. per-capita income is more than three times the Hopi number. Consistent with the low incomes received by Hopi people, rates of poverty on the reservation are relatively high. The following table presents economic data released by the Census Bureau:

	Percent of Individuals in Poverty
Hopis	41.6%
Arizona	12.8%
United States	12.7%

These figures indicate that the number of Hopis living below the poverty line is more than three times the rate for the United States as a whole and for Arizona. Data collected and released by the Hopi Tribal Council reveal an even greater disparity. According to the council's reports, more than half (56.5 percent) of Hopi residents are living below the poverty level. This figure is again substantially higher than the numbers given by the U.S. Census Bureau.

Data on employment also differ, depending on the source. The following table presents data collected by the U.S. Census Bureau for the year 2000:

	Percent Employed	Percent Unemployed	Percent Not in Labor Force
Hopis	41.2%	9.1%	49.7%
United States	67.2%	4.0%	32.8%
Arizona	62.2%	3.9%	32.3%

The data released by the Hopi Tribal Council use somewhat different criteria. According to its report, 40.4 percent of Hopis are fully employed, 15 percent are self-employed, 27 percent are unemployed, 6.8 percent have part-time or seasonal occupations, and 10.8 percent are retired.

Both sets of statistics reveal significant differences between the Hopis and other Americans. Whether compared with the general U.S. population or with residents of Arizona, the Hopis have significantly higher rates of unemployment. Employment rates are obviously related to income and poverty, since people who are unemployed or underemployed are more likely to be poor than working people.

Another indicator of economic and social difficulties is the housing stock on the Hopi Reservation. According to tribal sources, 68.1 percent of Hopi housing is in good condition, 29 percent have serious deficiencies, and 1.9 percent of the housing stock is characterized as dilapidated.

Despite the economic difficulties the Hopis face, the people strive to maintain their communities, knowing that their strength lies in their spiritual beliefs and practices and the continuation of their culture and language. Indeed, about two-thirds of the Hopis speak their Native language. According to the Census Bureau, 63.2 percent of Hopis speak the indigenous language, while 36.8 percent speak only English. And significantly, 21.3 percent of Hopis who speak both Hopi and English report that they speak English less than "very well." This means that for a large percentage of the Hopi population, all or nearly all of their daily conversations take place in the Hopi language.

Hopi officials and educators are involved in developing vigorous programs in the elementary and high schools that serve the Hopi community; aimed at maintaining and transmitting the people's culture, history, and language. The high school at Tuba City that serves both Hopi and Navajo students has instituted an innovative program stressing language and culture. Its goal is to encourage teenagers to be fluent in Hopi and to carry on their everyday conversations in their indigenous language. According to Dr. Harold Begay, associate superintendent of the Tuba City School District, interest in language maintenance is related to "tribal cultural renaissance":

> . . . you may also hear or may have heard quite often that our language and culture are priceless. With English education, learning their language and culture is not priceless, but rather it is extremely expensive in more ways than one, especially with us as Native peoples. There is a huge exacting cost incurred when we Native people lose ourselves in English education. As you go about the country, we often hear other nationalities converse with their young in

their Native tongue. But, with our Native peoples, we seem to make it a point to converse with our children in only one foreign language, the English language. Why? [We need to] dialogue on the value of our Native language and culture, not only for the present, but for years to come.

The Hopis have managed to endure more than four centuries of contact with foreign intruders and have been able to sustain their culture despite strong pressures to adopt Anglo ways. They have lived through many periods of economic and political hardship. Change in Hopi life has occurred, of course, as it has for all other people. But even though many Hopis now work in modern settings, speak English, and participate in local and national political movements, the Hopi philosophy of life remains strong and vital. This philosophy teaches the importance of balance and harmony. It stresses the strength of social ties among tribal members and the sacredness of spiritual bonds between human beings and all other creatures and forces in the universe. This philosophy has kept the Hopis strong for many past centuries and will no doubt keep the people strong for many centuries to come.

The Hopis at a Glance

Tribe	Hopi
Culture Area	Southwest
Geography	Northeastern Arizona
Linguistic Family	Uto-Aztecan
Current Population (2003)	11,323*
First European Contact	Francisco Vásquez de Coronado, Spanish, 1540
Federal Status	Tribal Reservation, established in 1882

* According to Hopi Tribal Council

c. 8000 B.C. Desert Tradition period begins in the Southwest of what is now the United States.

c. 3000 B.C. Desert people learn to grow their own food, mainly corn.

c. 1000 B.C. Desert people begin to grow new crops, including beans and squash.

300 B.C. Mogollon Tradition in the Southwest begins.

A.D. 1100 Anasazi Tradition begins in the Southwest.

1300s Large Anasazi villages are suddenly abandoned, perhaps due to climatic changes; the Hopis invent a new type of pottery; they begin to mine coal.

1350–1450 The Hopis leave settlement of Kayenta because of climatic change and drought.

1500s Historic period begins; foreign explorers arrive in Hopi territory.

1540 Franciso Vásquez de Coronado leads the first wave of Spanish exploration into Hopi territory.

1582 Antonio de Espejo leads a Spanish expedition through Hopi lands.

1598 Juan de Oñate leads the first group of Spanish colonists into what is now New Mexico.

1607 Oñate removed as governor of the New Mexican colony.

1609 Pedro de Peralta becomes governor of the New Mexican colony.

1629 Franciscan missionaries travel to Hopi villages and set up a mission.

1640s Severe drought hits Hopi territory.

1655 A group of Hopi representatives travels to Santa Fe to complain to the Spanish governor about a priest who had arrested a Hopi ritual leader.

1660s Another drought destroys Hopi crops and leads to food shortages.

Mid-1600s Epidemic diseases, including smallpox and measles, devastate the Hopi population.

1680 Pueblo leaders meet to come up with a plan to get rid of the Spanish intruders; they stage a rebellion—the unsuccessful Pueblo Revolt—in August.

1692 Spanish leader Diego de Vargas leads an army to Pueblo lands and takes control of villages.

1696 Large numbers of refugees flee Tewa villages; village of Hano founded.

1701 The Hopis attack the village of Awatovi for refusing to expel Franciscan missionaries.

1707 Hopis refuse to accept a Spanish visit.

1716 Hopis again refuse to allow Spanish into their villages.

1742 A Spanish traveler estimates the Hopi population at 10,846.

1775 Hopis reject a third Spanish attempt to infiltrate their lands.

1777 A period of drought and famine begins in Hopi territory.

1780 The Hopis refuse once more to allow the Spanish into the villages.

1821 Mexico wins independence from Spain.

1822 Santa Fe Trail opens, making Santa Fe a major trading center.

1824 Bureau of Indian Affairs (BIA) established.

1840 Trappers working for the Rocky Mountain Fur Company loot Hopi farms.

1848 Treaty of Guadalupe Hidalgo ends Mexican-American War; Pueblo Indian lands become part of the United States under the treaty's terms.

1850 BIA sets up regional headquarters in Santa Fe.

1851 U.S. government builds Fort Defiance in western New Mexico.

1853–1854	Smallpox epidemics strike the Hopis.
1858	Mormons begin to visit Hopi villages.
1861–1865	American Civil War.
1864	More droughts and waves of smallpox hit the Hopis; U.S. government begins policy to control the Navajos by fighting the tribe.
1870	Moravians set up a mission in the Hopi town of Oraibi; BIA opens an Indian Agency at Oraibi.
1870s	Construction of railroads brings a massive influx of non-Indian settlers to the Southwest.
1874	First government-run school opened for Hopi children; policy of forcing Native children to assimilate into white culture begins formally.
1875	Mormons set up a mission in Hopi village of Moencopi.
1878	Mormons build Tuba City, west of the Hopis' mesas.
1882	President Chester A. Arthur issues an executive order making Hopi lands a protected reservation.
1888	Polacca, a Tewa village, is founded at the foot of First Mesa.
1890	U.S. soldiers disrupt a Hopi initiation rite for boys and seize the boys, taking them away to government schools.
Late 1800s	A woman named Nanpeyo begins to revitalize the ancient Hopi craft of pottery.
1906	On September 8, differing factions among the Hopis hold a tug-of-war to decide who will stay in the town of Oraibi and who will leave; the so-called Hostiles lost and set up a new village for themselves.
1913	Hospital for treating Hopis and Navajos opens in Keams Canyon.
1920s	Government begins program of sheep-dipping to keep livestock from spreading infections.

1924   The U.S. government grants citizenship rights to all Native Americans.

1928   The Meriam Report, a national survey of conditions on Indian reservations, is issued.

1930s   BIA begins program to decrease the amount of livestock owned by Hopi and Navajo herders.

1933   Franklin Delano Roosevelt is elected president and makes John Collier head of the BIA.

1934   Indian Reorganization Act, which allows for some self-government on Indian reservations, is passed.

1935   A Hopi tribal council is elected.

1939   First Hopi high school opens in Oraibi.

1946   Indian Claims Court is founded.

1948   BIA opens the Branch of Relocation, with the intention to move Native Americans from reservations to cities throughout the United States in order to help them assimilate more quickly.

1950   Congress passes the Navajo-Hopi Act, which grants $88 million to improve both reservations.

1961   Hopi Tribal Council begins to lease land to U.S. companies that produce gas, oil, and minerals.

1966   Peabody Coal Company begins its controversial work on Hopi territory.

1970   Navajo Tribal Council offers to pay Hopis for the so-called joint-use area where both Hopi and Navajo people lived; the Hopis angrily refused.

1971   Ten Hopi villages file suit to stop the operations of the Peabody Company.

1974   Congress passes the Navajo-Hopi Settlement Act, which divided the joint-use area; the act was amended in 1978 and 1988 to redivide the area more equally.

1996 Congress passes the Navajo-Hopi Land Dispute Settlement Act, which updates the original law passed in 1974.

Late 1990s A severe drought takes place in the Southwest.

2002 Hopi tribal President Wayne Taylor, Jr., meets with Arizona Governor Janet Napolitano to discuss the Hopis' desire to have land held in public trust.

2003 Hopis sponsor a Water Fair at which researchers and activists from around the world discuss ways to protect and conserve water resources.

agent—A person appointed by the Bureau of Indian Affairs to supervise U.S. government programs on a reservation and/or in a specific region.

Anasazi Tradition—The way of life followed by the ancestors of the Pueblo Indians from around A.D. 1100 until the fourteenth century; Anasazi people transformed the culture of their ancestors to that of an urban society by creating elaborate systems of water control and building stone houses above ground, joined to each other, and having entrances in the roofs.

anthropology—The study of the physical, social, and historical characteristics of human beings.

Branch of Relocation—A Bureau of Indian Affairs program that helped Hopis obtain jobs in urban areas.

Bureau of Indian Affairs (BIA)—A federal government agency now within the Department of the Interior. Originally intended to manage trade and other relations with Indians, the BIA now seeks to develop and implement programs that encourage Indians to manage their own affairs and to improve their educational opportunities and general social and economic well-being.

culture—The learned behavior of humans; nonbiological, socially taught activities; the way of life of a group of people.

Desert Tradition—The way of life followed by the ancestors of the Pueblo Indians from around 8,000 to 300 B.C.; Desert people were nomadic and lived by hunting animals and gathering plant food but eventually learned how to grow crops.

District Six—The land area immediately surrounding the eleven Hopi Reservation villages that the Bureau of Indians Affairs' Hopi Indian Agency took charge of in 1943, effectively reducing the Hopi land base to only a little more than one-fifth of the reservation land that they had originally been granted.

Indian Claims Court—A federal court founded in 1946 to deal with Indian land disputes.

Indian Reorganization Act (IRA)—The 1934 federal law, sometimes known as the Wheeler-Howard Act, that ended the policy of allotting plots of land to individuals and encouraged the development of reservation communities; the act also provided for the creation of autonomous tribal governments.

kachinas—Supernatural beings associated with the spirits of ancestors, who are believed to live in mountains on the borders of Hopi territory; Hopi religion and worldview is centered on maintaining a proper relationship with the kachinas.

kachinvaki—The initiation rite, consisting of prayers and songs that teach about the spirit world, which Hopi children follow to become members of a kiva society.

kikmongwi—A town chief who gives advice and supervises the planning of village ceremonies.

kivas—Rectangular structures built completely or partially underground where Hopis meet for religious ceremonies.

lineage—A group of people who claim descent from a common ancestor.

matrilineal—Tracing lines of descent through the mother's lineage.

mesa—A flat-topped, table-like hill.

metates—Stones for grinding seeds and nuts.

Mogollon Tradition—The way of life followed by the ancestors of the Pueblo Indians from around 300 B.C. to A.D. 1100; Mogollon people transformed the culture of the Desert people by making pottery, building permanent dwellings, and learning how to plant more corps with more advanced agricultural techniques and tools.

Navajo-Hopi Settlement Act—A 1974 law that divided formerly joint-use land equally between the Navajos and the Hopis.

Niman—A festive dance in mid-July at which the Hopis bid farewell to the kachinas before their annual return to the spirit world.

piki—The cooking stone used to make wafer-thin blue cornmeal bread, also called piki.

Progressives—A group of Hopis who favored the modern style of elected representatives, in opposition to the Traditionals.

Pueblo Revolt—The first and only time in history that all the Pueblo Indians acted together, the 1680 revolt was intended to throw off the yoke of the Spanish; it succeeded in driving the Spanish out of New Mexico until the reconquest of 1692.

reservation—A tract of land retained by Indians for their own occupation and use.

Soyal—A December ritual performed to renew the earth and its life-giving forces.

Traditionals—A group of Hopis who sought to maintain clan chiefs as the legitimate local leaders and uphold tribal protection of the land.

tribe—A society consisting of several or many separate communities united by kinship, culture, language, and other social institutions, including clans, religious organizations, and warrior societies.

Bassman, Theda, Gene Balzer, and Jerry Jacka. *Treasures of the Hopi.* Flagstaff, Ariz.: Northland Publishing, 1997.

Benedek, Emily. *The Wind Won't Know Me: A History of the Navajo-Hopi Land Dispute.* Norman, Okla.: University of Oklahoma Press, 1999.

Courlander, Harold, ed. *Hopi Voices: Recollections, Traditions, and Narratives of the Hopi Indians.* Albuquerque, N.M.: University of New Mexico Press, 1982.

————. *The Fourth World of the Hopis: The Epic Story of the Hopi Indians as Preserved in Their Legends and Traditions.* Albuquerque, N.M.: University of New Mexico Press, 1992.

Dozier, Edward. *Hano: A Tewa Indian Community in Arizona.* Austin, Tex.: Holt, Rinehart & Winston, 1966.

James, Harry Clebourne. *Pages from Hopi History.* Tucson, Ariz.: University of Arizona Press, 1974.

Mails, Thomas E. *The Hopi Survival Kit.* New York: Penguin Books, 1997.

Malotki, Ekkehart. *Hopitutuwutsi or Hopi Tales: A Bilingual Collection of Hopi Indian Stories.* Tucson, Ariz.: University of Arizona Press, 1983.

Mullett, G. M. *Spider Woman Stories: Legends of the Hopi Indians.* Tucson, Ariz.: University of Arizona Press, 1979.

Ortiz, A., ed. *Handbook of North American Indians.* Vol. 9, *The Southwest.* Washington, D.C.: Smithsonian Institution, 1980.

Page, Susanna, and Jake Page. *Hopi.* New York: Harry N. Abrams, 1994.

Simmons, Don. *Sun Chief: The Autobiography of a Hopi Indian.* New Haven, Conn.: Yale University Press, 1942.

Smith, Watson. *When Is a Kiva? And Other Questions About Southwestern Archaeology.* Tucson, Ariz.: University of Arizona Press, 1990.

Stephen, Alexander MacGregor. *Hopi Journal.* Edited by Elsie Clews Parsons. New York: AMS Press, 1994.

Thompson, Laura, and Alice Joseph. *The Hopi Way.* New York: Russell & Russell, 1965.

Titiev, Mischa. *Old Oraibi: A Study of the Hopi Indians of Third Mesa.* Albuquerque, N.M.: University of New Mexico Press, 1992.

Udall, Louise. *Me and Mine: The Life Story of Helen Sekaquaptewa.* Tucson, Ariz.: University of Arizona Press, 1969.

Waters, Frank. *The Book of the Hopi.* New York: Penguin Books, 1977.

Whiteley, Peter M. *Deliberate Acts: Changing Hopi Culture through the Oraibi Split.* Tucson, Ariz.: University of Arizona Press, 1988.

Wright, Barton. *The Unchanging Hopi.* Flagstaff, Ariz.: Northland Publishing, 1975.

Wyckoff, Lydia L. *Designs and Factions: Politics, Religion, and Ceramics on the Hopi Third Mesa.* Albuquerque, N.M.: University of New Mexico Press, 1990.

Websites

Hopi Cultural Preservation Office
http://www.nau.edu/~hcpo-p

Hopi Kachinas
http://www.peabody.harvard.edu/katsina

Hopi Literature
http://www.indians.org/welker/hopi.htm

Navajo-Hopi Observer
http://www.navajohopiobserver.com

Official Site of the Hopi Tribe
http://www.hopi.nsn.us

Traditions of the Hopi
http://www.sacred-texts.com/nam/hopi/toth

page:

6: © Bob Rowan; Progressive Image/
   CORBIS
11: Library of Congress,
   LC-USZ62-113097
18: Library of Congress
25: © CORBIS
29: © George H. H. Huey/CORBIS
37: © CORBIS
41: Library of Congress,
   LC-USZ62-113098
51: Library of Congress Map Division
62: © CORBIS
65: © Underwood & Underwood/
   CORBIS

72: © Kevin Fleming/CORBIS
77: © CORBIS
82: Associated Press, AP/Roy Dabner
A: © Tom Bean/CORBIS
B: © Tom Bean/CORBIS
C: © Bob Rowan; Progressive Image/
   CORBIS
D: © Bob Rowan; Progressive Image/
   CORBIS
E: © Werner Forman/Art Resource
F: © Scala/Art Resource
G: © Werner Forman/Art Resource
H: © Branson Reynolds/Index
   Stock Imagery

Cover: © The Newark Museum/Art Resource, NY

Nancy Bonvillain, Ph.D., is currently a visiting faculty member in the summer session at Columbia University and teaches anthropology and linguistics at Simon's Rock College of Bard in Great Barrington, Massachusetts. She has written more than a dozen books including volumes in Chelsea House's INDIANS OF NORTH AMERICA series (*The Huron, Mohawk, Teton Sioux, Haida, Sac* and *Fox, Inuit, Zuni, Santee Sioux, Native American Religion* and *Native American Medicine*). And she has written two volumes of Native American biographies, *Hiawatha* and *Black Hawk*, in the NORTH AMERICAN INDIANS OF ACHIEVEMENT series.

Dr. Bonvillain's concentrations within the field have been in Native American studies and in linguistics. She has carried out fieldwork in the Navajo Nation in Arizona and the Akwesasne Mohawk Reserve in Ontario/Quebec and New York. Her dissertation was a study of the Mohawk language as spoken at the Akwesasne Reserve. She has also prepared a Mohawk/English dictionary and book of conversations for use at the schools on the reserve.

Ada E. Deer is the director of the American Indian Studies program at the University of Wisconsin-Madison. She was the first woman to serve as chair of her tribe, the Menominee Nation, the first woman to head the Bureau of Indian Affairs in the U.S. Department of the Interior, and the first American Indian woman to run for Congress and secretary of state of Wisconsin. Deer has also chaired the Native American Rights Fund, coordinated workshops to train American Indian women as leaders, and championed Indian participation in the Peace Corps. She holds degrees in social work from Wisconsin and Columbia.